TO HELL AND BACK

A Traveller's Guide

Carly Steadman

I dedicate this book to every person who is or has ever had to endure the immense burden of living with ME.

CONTENTS

'In oneself lies the whole world and if you know how to look and learn, the door is there and the key is in your hand. Nobody on earth can give you either the key or the door to open, except yourself.'

- Jiddu Krishnamurti

INTRODUCTION

Myalgic Encephalomyelitis (ME) is a seriously debilitating illness. It has been compared in its level of disability to multiple sclerosis and the final stages of cancer and yet, it is currently a highly misunderstood disease.

There is a widespread lack of recognition of the existence of the illness itself and that of its severity and complexity. For that reason, there is little respect being given to people living with ME, despite them having to endure a myriad of devastating symptoms on a daily basis. The general perception shared by medical professionals, strangers, and even friends and family is that this physiological problem is simply a psychological complaint. The very real and painful physical experience is minimised to that of a psychosomatic condition that individuals should be able to snap out of.

Speaking from my own personal nine-year battle, in addition to the many other experiences of people with ME that I have come into contact with, these unsympathetic and dismissive reactions can be more damaging than any of the harrowing physical symptoms there are to deal with. Having to cope with a serious disease is demanding enough on its own for anyone to manage. The struggle becomes infinitely harder when the support that is so desperately needed is not available.

This prevailing attitude also makes recovery very difficult. People with ME are frequently misdiagnosed or diagnosed too late, treated incorrectly and given treatments that only exacerbate their condition. Doctors tell them to push through their symptoms or use graded exercise and talk therapy. But more often than not, these prescribed remedies have the opposite effect to their intention, as they would with any other physical illness. These very real symptoms cannot simply be ignored or denied. I wish a cure could be that easy.

The label ME is only a blanket term that does not actually provide any tangible answers as to what is going on in the body to cause the dysfunction in the first place. The significant point here is that there *is* a reason for the pathology. There may be an array of explanations as to why each person is struck down with this host of matching symptoms. However, until the appropriate consideration is given and funding for research is provided, this vital information will remain shrouded in mystery.

Because of the immense lack of knowledge, right now there are no effective treatments for ME. Their absence is catastrophic to the millions of people who have contracted and been left to suffer with this chronic and often life-long condition. The illness has been documented to afflict approximately 17 million people worldwide. I believe this figure to be a gross underestimation of the true number living with the disease. To obtain a diagnosis is extremely difficult in a world where ME is trivialised and disregarded by the vast majority of medical professionals.

The widespread ignorance that exists within the medical system and beyond must no longer be tolerated. This illness needs to be recognised and respect given to the brave and resilient people who continue to suffer on their own, day in and day out. I wrote this book in order to share my story with as many people who will listen. Within its pages, I hope to illustrate how seriously incapacitating ME really is and to bring awareness to the importance of finding a real cause and cure for an illness that is currently being treated as if it doesn't exist.

To everyone out there who is a survivor of this disease: I salute you.

PROLOGUE
EIGHT YEARS IN

I lay in my bed 24 hours a day, completely still, with no aspect of outside life entering my tiny little world. I was devoid of touch, sound, daylight or any sight other than the occasional glimpse of my darkened room. Every so often I would muster up the energy to open my eyes in order to provide myself with the realisation that I was in my body, I was still human, I was alive.

I was completely trapped, restricted from making any movement, imprisoned within a self-imposed straight jacket. This entombment was a physical representation of the fundamental situation that I found myself in. I didn't get better. I didn't die. There was no way out for me, no chance of finding relief. I pleaded to the universe to be sent someone who could help me as I couldn't do it on my own. But no one else could either.

My existence had been filled with misery and darkness for so long now that I had forgotten about the light. It saddened me to realise how arduously I had struggled for so many years; all of the battles I had faced, the level of debilitation I had dealt with, the severe symptoms I had endured. I was shocked by how consumed I had become by the war that was raging inside of me, how starved I was of anything but this.

CHAPTER 1
THE BEGINNING

It was the summer of 2007 and my world as I knew it was about to come to a screeching halt. I was on the cusp of a life altering experience and yet had absolutely no expectations that anything out of the ordinary would happen to me. At the young age of 24 I could only picture my immediate future. I had no real thoughts that reached beyond this stage. Even if I had tried, I could never have imagined what was coming.

Up until that time I had what most would class as a pretty average life. I had grown up in a small town in South Florida with both of my parents and moved out on my own when I was 18. I had recently completed both of my degrees in psychology and social work and was now spending most of my days looking for employment from home. I felt excited about the prospect of finding a job in which I would help to support people with mental health issues as this had always been my passion.

After graduating from university, I had decided to take a trip to Costa Rica with a close friend in order to celebrate the milestone. We travelled around the country; discovering new places, visiting waterfalls and volcanos, zip lining and snorkelling. It was an amazing holiday until, on one of the last few days, I came down with sickness and diarrhoea. The vomiting only lasted for several hours but afterwards I was left feeling extremely ill and weak. Every time I tried to eat I would have recurring bouts of diarrhoea.

I returned home from the trip without seeing much of an improvement and, after a week, still couldn't stomach any food. At that time, I assumed that it was no more than a stereotypical case of traveller's diarrhoea. I made a visit to the doctor and was prescribed a week of antibiotics for a presumed bacterial infection. By the time I finished the course my health had returned back to normal and so I thought nothing more of what had happened.

However, over the next couple of months I began to experience occasional spells of exhaustion that could last anywhere from a few hours to the entire length of a day. During these times, my body would feel heavy and lethargic and I had very little energy. Whenever this occurred, I wanted to do nothing more than lay down and rest, but I would not allow myself to fully give in to what my body was telling me. In between searching online for jobs, I would take small breaks and lay on the sofa before pushing myself up and back to the computer again. I couldn't understand what was going on and wondered if I was becoming lazy after all of the weeks I had spent in the house.

One specific instance that stands out for me took place only a month after I had returned home from my holiday. To celebrate America's Independence Day, a couple of friends and I had decided to ride our bicycles down to a beach that was only a mile away from where I lived. On that day I ended up having one of my episodes of extreme fatigue. It began soon after we arrived at our destination. I tried to enjoy the time with my friends but found it quite difficult while dealing with my strong symptoms. The lethargy still hadn't passed by the time we left hours later. I was forced to walk my bike home slowly as I couldn't muster up the energy that was needed to pedal. When I finally made it to my flat, I collapsed on the sofa feeling completely drained and remained there for the rest of the evening.

After that, I began to take things a little more seriously but didn't feel any real concern. I presumed that I must be low in iron as by then I had been a vegetarian for over two years. I went to a vitamin shop and bought some supplements, believing that, once the nutrients had been given a chance to build within my system, the issue would resolve by itself. I will never know if those episodes of fatigue had anything to do with the following events. What I do know is that they were definitely out of the ordinary for me. Since I had never had any health issues before, it seems likely that they were in some way related.

The real beginning of this story doesn't take place until several weeks later when I became ill with what I thought was the flu. It began with all of the usual symptoms including the general malaise that the average person experiences when they have a virus. There was nothing to mention out of the ordinary. I followed the usual practice of resting and taking in lots of fluids and believed that it would be over in about a week's time. When seven days had gone by and I still wasn't feeling any better I didn't bat an eyelid.

It was at week three that my mum said to me that I should visit the doctor to make sure that nothing else was going on. Around that time, a friend told me that she had also been ill with a similar sounding virus that had taken her an entire month to recover from. After hearing her story, it seemed obvious to me that I had caught the same bug. I rarely became ill and had visited the doctor only a handful of times during my life. I had no reason to believe that I would have any real health concerns. But at the insistence of my mum I made an appointment anyway. I had complete faith in the medical system and associated going to the doctor's office with receiving a simple resolution to a physical complaint. The contrast between what I had experienced so far and what was about to take place would be considerable.

By this time, the initial flu symptoms of sneezing, congestion, sore throat and fever had disappeared. However, I was left completely drained and fatigued. I still couldn't manage to sit up for long and so would lay down in the living room all day. I had also developed a chesty cough and a macular rash over the lower half of my back which had not been present during the first couple weeks of my illness.

At the beginning of the appointment I told the physician that I had been ill with the flu, showed her the rash on my back and explained that I had been left feeling completely depleted all of the time. I couldn't manage to leave the sofa in the day and even simple activities like watching TV would quickly become too much. From this explanation alone, she became immediately convinced that nothing more was wrong with me than a case of the blues.

The doctor was adamant that I was depressed, even after I had replied very clearly to her that I was not, in any way, feeling even slightly low in mood. Hearing this only made her more determined to prove her point. She had never met me before that consultation and we had spent no more than five minutes together in the room. Yet she felt that she was more capable of determining my mental state than I was.

I was told that I was in a transition phase of my life since I had recently finished university. The woman then went on to explain that it was common to become depressed in these situations. I asked her, 'So when you are depressed you can feel physically ill?' Her answer was that yes, that could happen. I then questioned her about the rash covering my back. Her response to me was that it was a sun rash. When I told her that I had been too ill to leave the house for the last three weeks she simply repeated her conviction.

My patience began to dwindle. The physician was neglecting to listen to a word I had to say. I stated with unshakable certainty that I was completely content with my life and asked her point blank, 'So what you are saying is that you can actually be depressed when you are feeling happy?' She replied, 'Yes, this is possible.' In that moment, I felt so overwhelmed with frustration from having to listen to her ridiculous replies and condescending attitude. The last thing that the doctor said was that she would carry out some basic tests, but she did not believe that I needed them or that anything else, for that matter, was wrong with me.

I left the office feeling completely flabbergasted by the treatment I had just received. I had presented myself with real physical symptoms and yet had been told that my mental state was to blame for them. The way that the doctor had spoken to me had made me feel as though I was being accused of something. Although exactly what it was, I did not know. My first taste of that very crude response was preparation for the multitude of similar experiences that I would end up having with healthcare providers for many years to come.

I decided not to have any medical testing carried out with that particular physician. A couple of days later I sought out a second opinion from a separate doctor's office. Thankfully, during this consultation my mental state was never brought into the picture. I was, instead, treated as a medical patient with a physical problem. During my examination, the doctor noticed that I had swollen lymph glands in my neck which happens to be a common symptom of glandular fever. Because of this, it was included within the range of tests that were to be given to me. The preliminary blood test did indeed come back showing a positive result for the virus. Along with that, I also had a urinary tract infection. This seemed odd since I had no presenting symptoms and had never had a UTI before. I was given the usual prescription of antibiotics in order to resolve the problem.

The advice for glandular fever was to take plenty of rest, drink adequate fluids, follow a healthy diet and it would soon pass on its own. The nurse told me that I should come back for a second visit if I hadn't improved within a couple of weeks. She also mentioned that it wasn't unheard of for this particular illness to take a few months to completely disappear. I was already aware of the possible longevity from the stories that I had been told when I was younger. Someone I knew had to have her school work sent home for several months after contracting the virus as she had been too ill to attend. My idea was that it would take a little while for my body to heal but all I needed to do was be patient. And so I waited, all the while believing that I would soon be well and able to get on with my life.

Why would I think anything to the contrary? Soon after my diagnosis, I was discussing with a friend what I would do for my birthday which was a couple of months away. She asked me if I thought that I would feel better by that time. My reply was that *of course* I would. It was unfathomable to me that I could still be ill by then.

Unfortunately, my expectations never came to pass. When I returned to the doctor for my follow up appointment, I found out that my UTI hadn't resolved. It then took another full course of antibiotics to eradicate the infection. Six weeks after my initial visit, the office took another blood sample and reran some tests, but they simply came back with the same results. As there was no improvement to my exhaustion levels, the doctor wrote on my notes that I might have a condition called chronic fatigue syndrome. They never mentioned this to me and so I had no way of knowing about the prognosis at the time.

During this same appointment the nurse spoke with me about prescribing antidepressant medication. I felt confused as I couldn't understand why this was being offered as a treatment for glandular fever. She provided the explanation that the tablets have many benefits other than lifting mood, such as helping a person to stop smoking. In my naivety, I deduced that antidepressants must be able to heal glandular fever as well as improve a person's mental stability. I was unaware of the actuality that, yet again, a doctor was inferring that my illness was psychosomatic; mental factors were to some degree causing my physical symptoms or were even the sole reason for them.

During my childhood years, I had felt deeply loved and cared for and had always been treated with respect and kindness by both of my parents. In my opinion, this positive early start to life had helped me to become the balanced, happy, laid-back person that I was. I lived with the belief that if you wanted something badly enough, you went out and got it. Up until this point in my life I had been given no reason to doubt the future. To decide to take antidepressants when

I had no concerns with my mood did not sit right with me. As I was under the impression that it would only be a couple of months at most before I was well, I told the nurse that I would rather let the illness resolve itself naturally.

By this time, my cough and rash had cleared up, but I was still left with a pronounced general unwell feeling that I will call 'viral malaise'. The best way to illustrate this overlying symptom is to picture having a combination of a nasty flu and a permanent hangover. Although the description of how it feels is not perfect, it falls somewhere in that ballpark. I also suffered from a lack of energy and stamina. Because of this, whenever I attempted to do anything physical, it felt as though I was making my movements through a thick substance such as maple syrup or mud. This made all of my endeavours 100 times more strenuous. I would often break a glass when trying to drink my water simply because of how demanding it was for me to hold on to it. The muscle weakness and extreme fatigue would cause me to take hours to recover from doing anything seemingly simple such as making a sandwich or washing a few dishes. When I use the word 'fatigue' or 'exhaustion' or any other term of this nature to describe my symptoms, I am not referring merely to the feeling of needing to lay down in order to rest. During the energy depletion, it felt as though I was going to collapse; as if my battery had become completely flat. However, when I attempted to recharge it, my energy would only restore itself to a very weak level, no matter how long I rested for.

Another aspect of my functioning that had been severely affected was my cognition. I couldn't focus or concentrate on anything for very long without being completely drained of my energy. After speaking to someone for only a short time, my brain began to fail in keeping up with the new information and couldn't comprehend the words being said. I often had to ask people to slow down when they spoke to me and take their time when transitioning to new ideas as my mind was unable to make the switch easily. Word recall also became very taxing as I didn't have enough energy to think of the correct term. It was the same when trying to do basic maths. This was a surprise for me because I had always been very good with numbers. Nevertheless, the sheer brainpower that was required to compute anything was now too much for me to cope with.

Whenever I attempted any of these activities, my mind became so worn-out that I would have to have a period of complete rest and quiet in order to recover. Along with every other muscle in my body, my brain was exhausted. Two commonly used phrases that are used to describe this are 'brain fatigue' and 'brain fog'. I could relate to both as my head felt thick and unclear all of the time.

My cognition and fatigue issues were completely entwined. This meant that all of my cognitive abilities would worsen drastically after a period of activity, even following a physical action such as brushing my teeth or getting up to let my dogs into the garden. Conversely, if I used my brain for too long, my body would completely collapse. This curious phenomenon is called post-exertional malaise. Depending on how much I pushed myself over my limit, it could take minutes, hours, days, or even weeks to recover from a simple activity.

As well as becoming physically drained from the amount of energy it took to power my brain, I would also experience a headache unlike anything I had ever felt before. 'Painful' wouldn't exactly be the way to describe the sensation. It was almost like my brain was swollen. My head felt full, heavy and tight inside like it was about to explode with the pressure. As I rested, I could feel the vice-like grip begin to relax and loosen.

Not even my eyes were immune to the situation. When I became fatigued, everything I tried to look at would become out of focus. I had to stop reading after a short period of time as I could no longer make out the words on the page. Images on the TV screen would also become blurry only a short while after I began to watch a show. At these times, I was forced to close my eyes and rest them just as I did with every other muscle.

Because of the extremity of my symptoms my mum became

responsible for all of my household tasks, including cleaning, washing my clothes, taking care of my three dogs and making meals for me. At this stage, it wasn't considered to be out of the ordinary that I still had glandular fever. Despite knowing this, making it through each day was a struggle. All I wanted to do was to function normally again so that I could continue on with my life. I hated the fact that my healing was being drawn out so extensively. By the time I went to bed I was always relieved that the day had come to an end and I didn't have to lay looking at the ceiling any longer.

A few more months passed by and my health remained unchanged. I realised then that my current situation was going to last a little longer than the parameters of time that had first been suggested to me. I began to ask around in order to find out how long others had struggled with the virus for. On my search, I was told of a person in connection with my family who had suffered with it for two years before finally regaining his health. That was, by far, the longest period of time that I had heard of. Regardless of this new information, I was convinced that there was no way that I would be ill for that long. The story simply provided me with a time frame in which I did not have to worry. I had no explanation of why it was taking so long for me to heal, but I could now consider what was happening to me to be reasonable.

Life continued on in this fashion until eventually, after nine months had passed, I thought it would be wise to contact another doctor. I had decided to seek out one closer to home as journeys were now very difficult for me to handle.

During my initial appointment I shared information with the new practitioner regarding both the onset of the illness and my current symptoms. After listening to my story, she decided to do some more thorough blood tests regarding my glandular fever. In addition to the basic test that had been carried out before, she also ordered the Epstein-Barr virus antibodies test. Epstein-Barr or EBV is the virus that causes glandular fever. This test was more in depth. It looked at specific concentrations of different antibodies in my blood rather than simply stating a positive or negative. Each of the three levels that were tested for came back extremely high. To give you an idea of just how elevated they were I will share one of the findings with you. The result is considered positive if the score is over 120 AU/ml. Mine was 2,473 AU/ml.

My next interaction with the new doctor was to be another very unpleasant experience. After reading through my blood test results, she told me that I should stop wasting my life and get a job. She had seen people in much worse states than I was in and had patients with 'serious' illnesses like cancer. They were getting on with their lives and so why couldn't I? This last comment concluded our appointment.

After listening to the GP tell me with vehemence to get on with my life, I returned home feeling completely misunderstood all over again. These harsh judgements concerning my level of supposed laziness were painful for me to hear. What I had really needed in that moment was her unbiased professional guidance, but my medical situation had, instead, been totally disregarded. She was the second doctor that I decided I would not revisit again. At that time, I had no idea how long that list would eventually be.

From the doctor's limited explanation of the EBV test results, there was no way I could have understood their magnitude. I have since had physicians tell me that they have never seen such significantly raised results in all of their years of practice. Yet she had not even mentioned that they were remarkable in any way. The only information that I was given was that the new test confirmed what I already knew; I had glandular fever. I had never been given cause to doubt a healthcare provider before or to do my own research regarding my health. For that reason I trusted her limited explanation and thought no more about the findings.

Not long after that doctor's visit, I began to feel very restless. I had been told that I still had the virus and knew that all I could do about it was to wait. But nothing was changing, no matter how patient I was. The fact that there was no action for me to take in order to improve my circumstances was very difficult for me to accept. I was sick and tired of living out every single day staring up at that same ceiling. In my frustration, I came up with the idea to visit my father in England for six weeks. The desperate need to have a change of scenery was what gave me the courage to make the long trip.

From the minute that I left my house until when I arrived at my dad's, I had no idea how I was going to make it there. The first journey that I took in the car was already a struggle for me. When I arrived at the airport, the sounds and busyness completely overwhelmed me. It felt as though my brain was going to explode. I had to close my eyes and lay down in the terminal with my hands over my ears until my mum could check me in. Luckily, once this was done, I was able to wait for my departure gate to open within an empty room. After that I was taken directly to the aeroplane in a wheelchair. I then spent the entire flight slumping in an extended legroom seat while using an eye mask and ear plugs to shield me from my surroundings.

On making the decision to visit my father, I had naively believed that the long-term outcome of the visit would be worth the consequences of the flight itself. I saw it as a chance to breathe some new life into my world, which could help me to tackle my circumstances afresh. However, the travelling ended up depleting my body so severely of all of its reserves that it then took me my entire visit to recover. I had pushed myself way past my limits and, because of this, was forced to pay the price. Each day, I would lay on the sofa, on my own, in the quiet of my dad's living room, wishing that I had never come up with the foolish idea.

I had also envisioned that England's medical system might have other ideas about how to help me. Once I had recovered enough to start making occasional short trips out of the house, I made an appointment to see a GP. After listening to my story and giving me an examination, she then ordered many blood tests. Other than showing me what I already knew, the results also revealed that my erythrocyte sedimentation rate (ESR) was high. This finding indicates that there is inflammation or infection somewhere in the body. However, it does not specify what is causing the problem. I also had another positive UTI test, nine months after the first. Once more, it took a couple of courses of antibiotics to resolve the issue.

Each practitioner that I had seen so far had been unable to offer me a concrete explanation as to why I had been ill for so long. They would say things like; 'Everybody is different. Your situation happens in rare cases. You have to be patient' which I believed was true. Why would I have any reason not to? This doctor was the first to propose an idea. Her thoughts corresponded with the physician who had initially diagnosed me with glandular fever; that I may have chronic fatigue syndrome (CFS).

The diagnosis of CFS is given to a person when they present with fatigue as their main symptom and no explanation for it has been found. Up until this point I had never heard these three words strung together. I also had no knowledge of anyone having had an illness with an unidentifiable cause. I had been under the impression that whenever a person became ill, they could visit their GP and find out what was wrong with them.

Once I returned to the house, I got on the internet as soon as I could and read through numerous websites about the condition. I found so much information that appeared to parallel my specific circumstances, including descriptions of many of the symptoms that were affecting me on a daily basis. During the appointment, the doctor told me of a specialist service centre that I could attend that was near to where my dad lived. I was thrilled to be referred to a place that was treating people who were in the same state as me. I thought that once I became a patient there it would only be a matter of time before my health returned. This promising solution seemed to be the answer to all of my problems.

CHAPTER 2
I Wish I Could Be Like You

I still hadn't received my appointment letter for the chronic fatigue centre by the day I was booked to return to Florida. And so, I made the long, agonising journey home without ever having attended. I had never conceived that the referral could take longer to come through than the time I had left in the country. It was disappointing to me, but I accepted how things had panned out and continued to think, 'I will get better, it's just a matter of time.' If all I had been given to contend with was the waiting, my situation would have been difficult enough. But there were many more aspects to deal with than simply hanging around.

Whatever was happening to me had attacked my entire body, including my nervous system. Among other things, this is responsible for regulating the senses. From the beginning, I was extremely sensitive to my surroundings. I could handle a small amount of stimulation, but if it occurred over a longer period of time or at a higher intensity than I could bear, my energy became utterly depleted and my painful headaches would come on.

All my senses were affected, including sight, touch, and smell, but the most pronounced discomfort was caused by sound. I couldn't stand to be in a room full of people or be around any loud noises or busyness. I needed my world to remain quiet at all times. I could have a very limited amount of touch, but even this was taxing for me. I would tolerate a hug or a hand-hold here or there to please the caring people who wanted to share their affection. However, I wouldn't actually receive any pleasure from the exchange myself because of it being so physically draining for me.

I was unable to be around another person long enough to enjoy any real connection with them. Because of being starved of communication, whenever I had a visitor I would squeeze every last drop of energy out of my body in order to spend as much time with them as possible. The approximate hour that I rested on the sofa while chatting intermittently with a friend usually resulted in a couple of days of recovery time afterwards. In spite of this, I repeated the process as often as I could manage it as I judged the agony I experienced afterwards to be worth the pleasure of being in the company of someone else. These visits amounted to no more than one or two per month. There was nothing I could do except tolerate my symptoms and the lack of stimulation in the best way that I could. Sleep was also a major issue for me. I would lay awake for hours every night before managing to fall asleep. Once I finally did, at around 4am, I would then toss and turn, feeling very aware. By the morning I would have had about five hours of light sleep in total. I would wake up so tired that it felt as though I hadn't even been to bed. On top of feeling the exhaustion that was to be expected from having such unrefreshing sleep, I had hypersomnia. This condition caused me to feel as though I was drugged with a strong sleeping pill and made waking up a relentless struggle each morning. But if I gave in to the sensation, it would then take me even longer to fall asleep the next night.

The most unfavourable part of my day was always during the morning hours. Not only were my symptoms markedly worse at that time but I also had to face having a shower at the fastest pace I could manage. This was my most active pursuit in my minute daily agenda. I never knew how I was going to make it through those moments. My only strategy was to race through each step, skipping whatever I could to make the process run faster.

Another, rather odd condition that I had, called postural hypertension (PoTS), meant that whenever I stood or sat up my blood pressure would fall instead of increasing. Right from the start of the shower I could feel the dreaded fatigue, headaches and a desperate need to lay down building within me. As soon as the task was accomplished, I would collapse onto the sofa and then be immobilised for about three hours, all from that one activity.

Having PoTS made it impossible for me to sit upright for too long. If I tried, I would become light-headed and woozy. Although it was an improvement from standing, after about 15 minutes of sitting up, my energy would be completely depleted and the need to lay down would become unavoidable. Therefore, I was forced to lie on the couch almost all of the time, with pillows propped under me to create a small incline.

I was always looking for something to do in order to ease the monotony. These acts were never more strenuous than watching television for half an hour, reading for ten minutes or stroking my dogs for five. Despite this, I could feel my symptoms begin to build almost immediately. I would weigh each potential diversion up in my head beforehand, asking myself, 'Is the boredom I am experiencing now worse than how I will feel if I do something?' Quite often I would choose action over inaction. But of course, each time the terrible feelings of exhaustion came on, I would wish that I had rested instead.

By the end of each day, I would have perhaps watched a total of an hour of TV and read a few chapters in a book. That may have been all I did other than getting up to go to the toilet, get a glass of water or grab my ready-made meal from the refrigerator. Being unable to do more than a handful of menial activities made me feel an overwhelming sense of frustration and pointlessness. I wasn't accomplishing *anything*. I craved some purpose to my day, my week, my month, my life. All I could do was to focus on the notion that these troubles were only temporary.

About once a fortnight, out of pure desperation, I would make the effort to go out for some fresh air. My mum would pick me up after she had finished work and drive me around the corner to the beach as this was the most peaceful location within close proximity to my home. Even so, simply being in front of the ocean with its characteristic sounds and sensations, whilst contending with other visitors and cars going by, was too much for me to bear. After spending ten to fifteen minutes sitting quietly, the change in scenery would invariably result in me racing home in agony. I would then have to rest in solitude for hours or even days from my short outing. In the end I rarely left the house as I realised that the small amount of pleasure I received wasn't worth the terrible repercussions that followed.

Each evening, my mum would come over to my flat for a couple of hours after work to make me dinner and do any other household chores that were needed. Other than this short visit, I spent all day and night on my own in my apartment. After the first six months of this routine, we decided to move in together so that I could have more company. This adjustment also made it easier on my mum since she no longer had to take care of two households.

Despite making these changes, the new living arrangement didn't end up providing the benefit that I was craving. Life remained incredibly busy and stressful for my mum. During the weekdays, she would wake up early in the morning, work nine hours and begin her next full-time job of looking after me once she arrived home. There was a very limited amount of time to spare in which she could sit down and share a slow conversation with me. Unfortunately, my father, along with the rest of my family, lived far away in England.

At the same time, my relationships with friends were slowly dwindling. The trend followed in stages with the most distant ones withdrawing first. Then, gradually, I began to hear from my closer friends less and less. I could understand how this distancing had occurred as I was unable to sustain the friendships myself. I wanted them, I needed them, but I was only able to spend minutes at a time within their presence. I could also see how having an ordinarily full and eventful life would make it difficult for my healthy friends to remain in contact with me. Being aware of all of this still didn't lessen the level of loneliness that I felt. This limited contact with others was one of the most upsetting aspects of my condition.

I lay in wait and watched on as my friends' and family members' lives progressed. It felt okay at first, but after a while I began to sense that I was missing out on something. When I was asked to be a bridesmaid at one of my best friends' weddings, I knew that I had to be there, no matter what. I was aware that the undertaking would be demanding, but I didn't care. I was not going to miss this meaningful event. It wasn't until a few weeks beforehand, when I was having my dress altered by a family member, that the seriousness of what I was about to do became inescapably obvious. The simple act of trying the outfit on and then standing up for several minutes while she pinned it in all of the right places took me the rest of the afternoon to recover from. I began to wonder how I was ever going to make it through the actual ceremony.

On the day, I arrived at the venue and went straight into a quiet room on my own, lying my head on the table until it came time for me to walk down the aisle. Another member of the wedding party then supported me to the special seat that was waiting for me near the altar. This is where I sat while the vows were being spoken. When the service finished, with assistance, I made it back up the aisle before collapsing.

I attempted to stay at the reception for a while, using earplugs to drown out some of the noise. However, it quickly became paramount that I leave the celebration as I couldn't stand the intensity of it all. On my way home I felt a mixture of emotions: happiness to have been able to be a part of my best friend's wedding day but also such disappointment that I had been forced to leave before all of the fun that followed afterwards. I hadn't seen the first dance or the cake being cut. Neither did I hear the speeches or party the night away with all the other guests.

One day, after I had been ill for around a year, a friend from the past phoned me and asked if he could pop by. I wanted so badly to feel like a normal person during our visit. When he arrived, I made the decision that *I* was going to put some demands on my body that day, rather than it on me. My friend drove me to a cafe right around the corner for lunch. I sat upright and held a conversation with him for a full half an hour. I did not take breaks and acted like I was fine, even though inside I felt as though I was dying. For the first time, I completely ignored my body's pleas. In that moment, my need for genuine connection outweighed any discomfort that I felt.

The level of agony that I had experienced while continuing to try and enjoy myself was nothing compared to the impact my actions had on me the next morning. With post-exertional malaise, the full physical repercussions can come on hours or days after the actual exertion has been carried out. Because of this, it had always been very difficult for me to know precisely when to stop an activity. Following that visit, I was shown the true power that aspect of my condition could wield.

The ramifications hit me instantly upon waking. My energy was depleted beyond belief, my sensitivities to sound and sight had become ten times worse than they had ever been and my head felt like it would explode from the unbearable pressure. I could not move from my bed. It is very hard to put into words the magnitude of what I was feeling in that moment. All I can do is assure you that it was not in the least bit pleasant.

I was able to get out of bed again after about a week, but it took an entire year for me to fully recover from this relapse. When I use the word 'recover' I mean that my body gradually made its way back to the pre-existing level of debilitation that it had been in before the day that I made that grave mistake. These excessive repercussions had been caused by no more than a couple of hours spent talking to an old friend while sitting within an average cafe. It was only after this instance that I learned the true importance of listening to everything my body was telling me at all times.

My health never moved beyond my baseline no matter how much I rested. If I took care, I was able to make small improvements to it. But they were made in such tiny increments that it would take months to notice them. And then some out of the ordinary, seemingly small event would happen and I would find myself back to zero again. The patience that was required for me to maintain my composure in this never-ending battle was slipping.

Just over a year into my illness I gave in and bought a wheelchair. I felt embarrassed about having to rely on a mechanical contraption to move around but tried to focus on the idea that it was only a temporary solution. I realised that the device was a necessary evil as it enabled me to get to places when needed. It also afforded me a change of scenery and some fresh air every now and again. Up until this point I hadn't been able to go anywhere other than in the car, as I did not have the energy it took to walk further than the length of a bus. With the use of a wheelchair, I could now move through my surroundings, although watching the scenery pass by was an overload on my senses. My mind didn't have the capacity to compute each new object, colour or changing light level. Because of this, my trips out had to remain very short.

Not long after the wheelchair purchase, I caught a cold and went on to develop a very bad cough. It became so extensive and forceful that I ended up hurting several of my ribs and upper back on my right side. From then on, these areas were so tender that when I tried to lean even slightly backwards the position would cause me excruciating pain. I had to keep all weight off of the affected ribs and could no longer use my right arm at all. Being able to find a comfortable posture to rest in became a thing of the past. Although the severity of the pain subsided somewhat over time, this discomfort persisted for the entirety of my illness.

On top of the wide assortment of symptoms that I had started with, new ones were constantly popping up. The list was ever growing. Each time this happened I would have to readjust to managing with the recent addition as it became a permanent facet of my condition.

The next one to surface rather suddenly, was what I suppose could be classed as irritable bowel syndrome. From that point on, I could only tolerate eating bland food. Even then, I would frequently have terrible stomach aches and diarrhoea. As a result of receiving insufficient nutrients, I quickly began to feel even more weak and lethargic than I already had.

During this difficult period of time, I was invited to my father's wedding in Jamaica, not so far from home as my last trip. I knew how much it would mean to him for me to be a part of the celebration and so I decided to go. A few days before leaving for the special occasion, my stomach became so irritated that I was only able to eat three foods: dry toast, white rice and bananas. That small selection of ingredients constituted my entire diet from the beginning to the end of the trip. Even on this limited diet my diarrhoea was unremitting.

My hotel room was shared with another family member who, luckily for me, was incredibly sweet and understanding of my embarrassing situation. One evening, in order to put my mind at ease, she relayed a personal story that had taken place while she had been on holiday to a developing country. During her travels she had come down with food poisoning and, while out exploring one day, had actually 'sharted'. At this point in her story a baffled look came over my face as I had never heard that word before. It was then that I was informed of the term's meaning: a person farts but unexpectedly to them, the action releases a little more than they have bargained for. Hearing her story made me chuckle but more importantly, it also helped me to feel a little less self-conscious about my condition.

Low and behold, the next morning I was in my hotel room, minutes away from leaving for home, when suddenly I had my own personal 'sharting' experience. There could not have been a more humiliating coincidence. I had no idea what to do; the mess, the smell, the embarrassment, mixed with my total surprise. I had to think of some way to discard the evidence, but how? I ended up screwing my knickers into a ball and leaving them in the rubbish bin for my roommate to smell later. Not very discreet I realised, but the best I could come up with in the few minutes I had left. That story was included, not only to lighten the mood a little, but also to give you an idea of just how sensitive my stomach was.

The average healthy person will have diarrhoea intermittently throughout their lives which may last a few days, or a week at a stretch. Eventually the symptoms subside, and with that, they are able to resume a normal diet. My predicament continued for a total of 12 months. Thankfully, in the end the condition cleared up on its own and I was then able to eat whichever foods I wanted to again. The freedom of choice felt so wonderful after I had spent an entire year eating such a tiny selection. As the variety of nutrients I was able to consume increased, so too did my strength and energy levels. Although I was appreciative of these positive changes, my physical health was nowhere close to where I yearned for it to be.

Eventually, after almost two years of struggling on our own, my mum and I decided to move back to England. Relocating to another country marked a new beginning in my mind. I thought that if I changed my external environment, there was a possibility that something would change in my internal environment. A fresh start might spark my body to move into recovery. We chose to go to Oxfordshire as most of my family on my mum's side was there along with her old friends.

Once we were there, I was rarely able to speak with my American friends anymore. This was back in the dark ages before apps made it possible to phone around the world for free. Every time I did manage to have a short phone conversation with someone, they would always ask me, 'So have you made any new friends yet?' What they didn't understand was that there was no conceivable way for me to do this. I hadn't thought the scenario through properly beforehand, having focused on the assumption that soon after my return I would make a full recovery and be able to move forward in creating my new life. Unfortunately, this nightmare was going to be drawn-out for much longer than I had envisioned.

My illness had always been trivialised by everyone, including my closest friends and family members; those with the best intentions. Nothing changed in this respect once I lived in England. Some people went as far as to insinuate that there was nothing wrong with me at all. Because of their preconceived notions, they assumed that either I was fabricating something in my mind or that I didn't want to get on with life and was making an excuse to opt out. Their convictions were exceptionally strong and they made sure to voice them to me regularly.

The first clear example of this that I can remember occurred one evening after I had been confined to my house for several months. On this occasion, a friend had stopped by for a short visit on her way home from work. I stood talking with her for a couple of minutes, feeling the dreaded depletion coming on. The conversation began with her asking me a seemingly innocent question. She wanted to know why I was unable to function normally. When I had answered her, she followed on by saying that sometimes she felt exhausted too with the stress of holding down a job and taking care of a house, but she realised that it had to be done.

This comment was upsetting for me to hear but it was the next statement that really got to me. With a coldness in her tone she said 'I wish that I could be like you and do nothing all the time.' As if I had a choice. As if the only reason that I lay down in my house all day long, completely alone, doing absolutely nothing, was because I wanted to. Hearing that this was how a close friend viewed my situation was very painful. Her insensitive remark was just a taster of what was to eventually be administered in bucket loads.

I felt thoroughly misunderstood and so alone in the world; like an outsider, which only compounded the intensity of the isolation that I already had to deal with. I was constantly trying to prove to everyone that I did in fact feel ill. No matter what I said I couldn't make myself heard. No one, save for my mum, could appreciate all that I was going through. Others would see me during the fifteen minutes or so when I was ignoring my symptoms in order to share a short conversation with them. Yet, they weren't there to watch as my body collapsed in my room after being in their presence. They never witnessed the hours, days, or weeks that it would take for me to recuperate fully; all of the time that I spent laying silently in bed, willing myself back to my baseline.

My illness had very few outward signs. Anyone else who has been afflicted with CFS will be familiar with the frequent comments that I received from people I knew or even those I had just met, including, 'You don't look ill' and 'I can't see anything wrong with you.' These were said in a disbelieving tone, along with other similar remarks, inferring that because I looked fine on the outside, this proved that there was nothing wrong with me.

Even those who trusted that my illness was genuine were convinced that at least an aspect of it was psychological. I was constantly being given advice that completely belittled all that I was contending with. These individuals would say that if I just got back out into the world and got on with my life it would all disappear. Time and time again I heard, 'Why don't you go and get a job' or 'just take a walk' or even once 'a run' in order to fix everything.

It was the tone in which the words were articulated that made them so offensive. They never came with any empathy or even so much as sympathy. Neither were they provided in an attempt to try and understand. Instead, they were produced with a chuckle, or a smirk and in a mocking or judgemental tone. These highly opinionated people seemed to feel that they knew better than myself what I was going through. After hearing comments such as these repeated over and over, they began to wear me down. Over the years I would become annoyed, frustrated, infuriated, and eventually weary of it all. It quickly became obvious to me that the move itself was not going to produce the shift in my health that I had hoped for. My focus then turned to the new and promising medical care that I imagined I would receive. I held high hopes for the first doctor I visited, thinking that she may have some fresh ideas. I was also excited about the possibility of being put in touch with a CFS service centre again, like the one I had been referred to the year before.

Sadly, my next healthcare experience was to be on par with all of the previous ones I'd had. After rushing me through a description of my symptoms, the latest GP took one look at me and my American doctors' notes and made a decision right then and there; that there was nothing wrong with my health and whatever was happening was all in my head. Her implication was made clearly evident by the way she spoke to me with outright disrespect and disdain in her voice during the entire appointment.

After listening to my condensed synopsis, the new doctor asked me in a scathing tone, 'But you walked from the car to the office, didn't you?' This happened to be true. However, the action had taken me only about twenty steps which, at that time, I was just about able to manage. I naïvely assumed that, after reading my Epstein-Barr virus test results, she would be able to acknowledge that there was something dysfunctional happening in my body. As soon as she had looked them over, the GP told me with a palpable level of disdain that there was no meaning to the results before her as a test of that depth did not exist. She claimed that the only marker for glandular fever was the one that provided a simple positive or negative test result.

My response to her was posed in the form of a question: If that was so, how could my American doctor have explained these results within the context that she had? The physician refrained from answering but instead told me matter-of-factly that the virus would have disappeared from my body by now anyway. Therefore, there was no possibility that it was still causing any lasting effects. My energy should be focused on getting back into the world and starting to live again.

The last remark she made had completely minimised and disregarded the serious situation that I was in. All I wanted to do was to get better. Every fibre of my being wished that I could follow the GP's advice, but it was impossible. How wonderful it would have been if the answer was that simple; just get off my bum and start living again.

This heartless reaction, shown to me by yet another physician, felt extremely disappointing and frustrating. I didn't know what I could possibly do to make myself heard when no one within the medical profession would make any effort to listen. How was I ever going to get the help that I needed if doctors didn't believe that there was anything physically wrong with me?

With that realisation I decided to inform the woman about the condition of chronic fatigue syndrome having been mentioned to me in the past. After doing my own research online, I believed that the diagnosis was warranted. My presumption was that if this doctor could make this official, I would then be provided with the treatment that I needed to get better. Once she had finished thoroughly questioning my reasoning and listening to my affirming replies she said, 'You realise that this is a serious diagnosis?' I nodded my head. It was at that moment that the label 'chronic fatigue syndrome' became a permanent addition to my medical file.

Little did I realise, when pushing to have those three words added to my records, that this action would be sealing my fate. So often, doctors will give a diagnosis of CFS to their patient as an excuse to stop searching when really there is an underlying cause to the fatigue that still needs to be found. Generally, once this label is in place, the interpretation is viewed as conclusive. The name 'chronic fatigue syndrome' doesn't help matters either. Emphasising the fatigue completely minimises the multitude of symptoms and the level of pain and hardship that people who fit into this category must face daily. Using the word 'syndrome' makes the illness sound more psychological than physical in nature. Therefore, it has less of a chance of being taken seriously within a medical setting. Before receiving my diagnosis I had thought that, once doctors could see the label CFS on my chart, they would become committed to finding a cure. In the months to come I would find out that nothing could have been further from the truth.

A few months after that doctor's appointment, the safety net of my self-imposed two-year time frame passed by. With that, I officially became the longest account of a person afflicted with glandular fever that I had ever heard of. This was when I began to feel highly concerned and, as a result, immediately became proactive. I went online to try and find any other illnesses that matched my symptoms. It wasn't long into my search before I came across a website describing something called Myalgic Encephalomyelitis (ME). It was the first time I had heard of the condition, and I identified with it straight away.

ME and CFS are closely linked as they share the common bond of having unexplained fatigue as their main symptom. They are also both mystery illnesses; a label put on a set of symptoms that have no explanation. However, there *is* actually a difference. A diagnosis of CFS can be given when a person has unexplained fatigue for more than six months that reduces their functioning to fifty percent or less. That is all of the criteria that is needed for that specific label. ME is a more comprehensive diagnosis that also includes post-exertional malaise with prolonged recovery time and central nervous system dysfunction including autonomic, cognitive, and sensory disturbances amongst its requirements (*M.E or CFS?*, 2006-14). All of these were symptoms that I experienced on a daily basis.

People, including those in the medical profession, often incorrectly use the two names interchangeably. Because of a lack of knowledge, it is also common for someone to be misdiagnosed with CFS when they really have ME. Although these labels represent two distinguishable entities, for the ease of reading I will from now on use the term ME to represent my personal experience and that of all others who are able to closely relate to it, many of whom have been given the diagnosis of chronic fatigue syndrome.

The literature I read on ME fit me to a tee. I related emphatically to the symptoms but, more importantly, to the many stories sufferers shared of how frustrating the illness was and how they were rarely ever believed or listened to. They talked about the discrimination they faced so often by doctors, strangers, friends, and family. The same remarks had been made to them as what I had endured, the same expectations, the same disdain, ridicule, and disrespect. These people felt isolated, lost, and confused and yet there was absolutely no support out there, nowhere to turn. All of their comments resonated very strongly with me, and I was able to find some sort of solace in their words. Although I would have never wished this awful disease on anyone, it felt comforting to know that there were other people in the world who had experiences that resembled my own.

CHAPTER 3
PILLS AND POTIONS

One of the few similarities that ME shares with chronic fatigue syndrome is that there are no traditional medical treatments currently available. Once I had learned everything that I could about the illness, I promptly began to do research on various alternative remedies. I put every ounce of my energy towards the pursuit. During this slow, drawn-out search I came across an advertisement for a specialist centre located in London. The man who owned and ran it had actually had ME for years before making a full recovery. He asserted that others could do the same by following his regime. This mainly consisted of nutritional and psychological approaches, the latter focusing on using mind over matter techniques in order to create physical healing.

I was willing to consider that the human mind could be powerful enough to affect positive change within the body. Over the years I had heard rare stories of people who had made full recoveries from serious, life-threatening illnesses in this manner. After reading many positive testimonials on the centre's website, I decided that it was definitely worth a shot. I chose this avenue over asking my doctor to attend a CFS clinic as the place addressed ME specifically.

Within the six months that I had been living in England my baseline had increased ever so slightly. When I say this, I am talking marginally. For example, I had now become able to hold a conversation once a day for around 20 minutes without having serious repercussions. After taking a shower, my recovery time was down from three hours to two. I was also able to sit up for about half an hour and to walk for about a minute without collapsing. There were other small changes on par with these. I had nowhere near the level of stamina that was required for me to attend the centre but, regardless of this, was adamant that I would go. I rationalised that I would be present for as much of it as I could as I was convinced that the programme was what would make me well.

Becoming a patient there marked my first endeavour in my independent search for healing and provided me with the biggest hope that I had been given so far. The course consisted of three whole days in which participants would learn how to support and heal themselves. Upon arriving, I met nine other people who also had ME and were struggling to find an answer. The amount of time that they had been ill ranged from one year to over 20. Hearing that some of them had been living with their symptoms for decades was a very frightening discovery. In that moment, I was alerted to both the seriousness and potential longevity of my circumstances. Although I felt the beginnings of my budding concerns, I assured myself that this unnerving story would never become my own.

I connected with the members of the programme very easily. This was because, even though my baseline was noticeably lower than everyone else, all of our main symptoms were the same. No one questioned whether there was a real physical reason for me withdrawing each time I had to leave the room or if what I was experiencing was truly as intense as I was claiming it to be. It was the first time that a group of people had fully appreciated and respected my needs and feelings which was a revelation for me.

All of the other participants were able to make small talk with one another during the length of the course. Some of them even held part-time jobs. For me, simply being around the noise of their intermittent chatter was a struggle. I had my speculations about why I was the only person needing to repeatedly retreat from it all. When booking my place on the course, I had knowingly lacked the energy that was necessary to participate in the three days and yet had decided to go anyway. I was only in that room because I was willing to push myself beyond my limits and risk a relapse in order to have my first serious chance of healing. Perhaps, in general, other people in my position weren't quite as head-strong (or as foolish, depending on how you looked at it).

During the course, we were taught various techniques on how to 'believe ourselves well'. The programme worked with the theory that all chronic illnesses manifest themselves when a person is overwhelmed by some aspect of their lives. We were told that if a person learned to deal with these stressors in a healthy way, any sort of malfunction within the body could be restored. The facilitators explained that people with ME fit into one or more of three categories; anxiety types, achievers and helpers. To address the anxiety types, they taught everyone relaxation techniques. For the helper types it was to focus on ourselves before helping others and to develop the ability to say no. For the overachievers it was to work on no longer needing to accomplish something in order to feel worthy.

In addition to the standard relaxation techniques, we were shown specific methods to support us in overcoming our collective anxiety regarding our illnesses. No one within our group was exempt from that stressor. We focused on letting go of the fears we faced every day in deciding whether a physical or mental activity was going to cause a drop in our baselines. We were also taught how to try to conquer our fear of the disease in general. The class was told to put a stop to negative thoughts such as, 'I will never get better.' In their place we were instructed to say to ourselves that we were in the process of healing. Instead of telling people that we were ill, we were to say that we were recovering.

The programme also addressed one of the main symptoms of ME;

the 'wired but tired' state. The condition had come on suddenly when my illness began and, for over two years now, I had been struggling daily with racing thoughts. Just to clarify, this was not anxiety but hyperactivity. It felt like I had too many cups of coffee, even though I never drank it. No matter how hard I tried, I could not be still, calm or focused. Even a normal healthy person would have felt drained by the relentless whirling thoughts. Living constantly in this unnatural state stole away any small amount of energy that I had left.

Instead of winding down towards the end of the day, my mind would grow ever more wired as the night progressed. When I went to bed I would remain awake until the early hours, feeling completely exhausted but not in the least bit sleepy. Even when I woke up groggy in the morning, my mind was still able to race. The sensation persisted day and night for all the time that I was ill. The London centre attempted to address this by teaching us to stop in these moments and become conscious of our breath. Although I followed these directions religiously, I found this psychological method to be ineffective in battling a symptom that was caused by a physical condition.

The facilitators taught us that to conserve energy, we should withdraw from an activity as soon as we saw a negative reaction begin and take the rest that was needed. This technique is called pacing. I learned to become aware of what my body was telling me in every moment and to cultivate a deeper respect for its messages. This technique would become very beneficial to me over the time that I was ill. However, it was not without its drawbacks. Because of how extremely ill I was, almost all of my day was now taken up by doing nothing other than resting my broken body. Before I learned about pacing, I had often pushed myself too far, but I had created this pattern for a reason. Each time that I had ignored my waning energy levels it had given me a few extra minutes of enjoyment. All of my attention was now focused on doing what I believed it would take to get well, at the detriment of receiving much less gratification from the present moment. The level of energy and stress it took for me to follow the entire treatment plan was enormous but I put my whole heart and soul into it, never once veering from their instructions.

The other half of the programme involved seeing a nutritionist. After my first appointment, the practitioner ran many tests to look at the functioning of my stomach and the nutrient levels within my body. Within my test results, it was plain to see that my adrenal glands were struggling; a common finding in people with ME. These are the organs that are responsible for producing cortisol; the hormone that helps us to manage stress and metabolise sugars and fats from the food that we eat. My daily cortisol level was just 12.9 nmol/L. The finding was considered to be very low as the normal reference range was between 21 and 41. My nutritionist informed me that this abnormality was the causal factor of my racing thoughts and issues with sleep. I was given a supplement to take to support my adrenal glands and told that continuing with the psychological side of the program would help me even further.

It had also been found that I was having difficulty absorbing protein. This had the added effect of destabilising my blood sugar levels. I craved meat, fats and satisfying foods all the time. The symptoms even came on in the middle of the night. Quite often, I would wake up feeling hungry and woozy and need to eat something high in protein to get back to sleep. I began leaving food such as nuts by my bedside to save me the extra effort of getting myself out of bed to find something quickly. I was advised to avoid foods that had a high glycaemic index. Even seemingly healthy ones such as bananas and beetroot were included on the 'no' list.

I began to follow a special diet in which I cut out dairy, wheat, yeast, processed products and refined grains and sugar. Because of my inability to absorb protein properly, it was also recommended that I stop being a vegetarian. This was a difficult decision for me to make. By that time, I had been following the diet for five years because of personal and deeply held principles. Giving it up didn't feel like a choice but rather another aspect of myself that the illness had taken away. In doing this, I was letting go of a big part of who I was. I decided to follow the nutritionist's guidelines, believing that if I did everything she said I would soon be well and could then resume my vegetarian lifestyle.

Further testing revealed that I had leaky gut syndrome; a condition caused by a more serious level of candida overgrowth. Candida is a fungus which, if allowed to proliferate, weakens the digestive and immune systems. It causes fatigue, headaches, brain fog, irritable bowel syndrome and food intolerances among other symptoms. After being tested for specific intolerances, I was given a long list of foods to avoid. From then on, everything that I wanted to eat had to be analysed. Nine times out of ten, if the product in question had more than one ingredient, it would contain something that was deemed to be harmful to me. The strict diet I had to follow became a bit of an obsession. If I ate an inappropriate food by accident and then found out about it, I was devastated. By this point, the centre's protocol was the only hope that I had to hold on to.

It seemed that everything in my life had been either cut back, made bland or taken away completely. Having ME continuously starved me of any pleasure. I presume that anyone who has lived with it would say the same. It had stripped me of so many aspects of my life; of the company of others, of enjoyment, of being carefree, food was just another one. I had been forced to become aware of everything I was doing; to check myself, to check how I was feeling, to check ingredients, check, check, check.

My secretory IgA was another test result to come back abnormal. This important antibody is central to the functioning of the immune system as it defends the body from harmful pathogens such as viruses, bacteria, parasites and yeast. Its normal reference range is between 51 and 204 mg/dL. My score was only six. One more bottle of pills was added to my never-ending list in order to try and combat this imbalance. I was taking 14 different kinds of supplements in total, at multiple times throughout the day. A giant container, approximately double the size of a shoe box, was kept underneath the table next to where I lay, filled with the various pills, liquids and powders that I had been advised to take.

At the time of my first nutritional consultation, my prolonged episode of diarrhoea had been over for almost a year. Within a few months of taking the considerable number of vitamins and following the strict diet plan that had been prescribed to me, my stomach was up to its old tricks. Once again, it had started to react to a high percentage of the foods that I ate and with that, the frequent bouts of diarrhoea returned with a vengeance. For days after each incident I would be forced to eat only bland foods until my stomach balanced out.

I was distraught to find myself back in this all too familiar territory after spending the last year being able to eat whatever I wanted. This time, although the severity of the condition fluctuated, it became a permanent feature of my illness. Looking back, I have the opinion that my stomach simply couldn't cope with the many rules and regulations and pills and potions that were thrown at it all at once.

Sadly, both the psychological and nutritional methods of the program had absolutely no positive effect on my health. Other than learning how to pace my activities, I received no benefit from attending the three-day course or from the appointments with my nutritionist. Not one of the 14 supplements ever made any difference. After investing my time, energy and money in the London centre for a full year, I was no further along in my quest to get well. I decided to look elsewhere.

I made up my mind that my next step was to attend one of the CFS service centres that I had been hopeful about going to two years previously. When I received my appointment date, I felt a renewed sense of excitement about the chance I was being given.

A nurse was sent out to the house as I was too ill to visit the site myself. During her visit I told her about my symptoms and how unbearable they were for me. I also described my isolation and how exhausting it was to participate in conversation. I was having to push myself beyond my limits to gain the most out of the consultation that I possibly could, knowing full well that I would have to pay for the extra exertion later. I put all of my hopes in her expertise, believing that the more she knew about me and the more I learned from her, the higher chance I would have to become well.

At the end of the discussion, the nurse's only comment to me pertained to something she said she had observed; that there was an inconsistency between the way that I had described the severity of my symptoms and the amount of talking and listening I had done during our time together. She then suggested that I consider what this meant. I was astounded that these were her pearls of wisdom. I had hoped for so much more from a place that was meant to be competent in their knowledge and treatment of CFS and ME.

The specialist spent the rest of the visit describing the three standard treatment methods included within the clinical guidelines of the National Institute for Health and Clinical Excellence (NICE) and currently endorsed by the National Health Service. The first technique, called graded exercise therapy, asserts that if someone with CFS/ME gradually builds upon the intensity and length of their physical and mental activities over time, they will be able to heal completely. Nothing could be further from the truth. I say this from my own personal experience but also from speaking with many other individuals with ME. No one has ever told me that doing more, no matter how gradually, helped them in any way, shape, or form. I have, however, spoken with a substantial number of people who have relapsed after using the technique.

There is a physical reason for why their bodies stop functioning properly, which makes it impossible for them to simply push through the disease using increasing amounts of activity. No one would tell a cancer patient to shrug off their symptoms and build up their strength with exercise, just like no one would inform a person with AIDS that if they take an incrementally longer walk every day, they will eventually be well. This advice could be beneficial once the disease has been eradicated from the body. However, during the time that an element is attacking and weakening it, the worst thing a person can do is to force themselves to undertake a higher level of activity than they are able to cope with.

It is shocking to me how little these medical professionals base their convictions on actual evidence. PACE, the renowned research study that impacted the wide acceptance of graded exercise, was later found to have produced biased results. This was because of the way its participants had been chosen. To become a part of the study, someone only needed to display the symptom of non-specific fatigue. This allowed for the inclusion of a myriad of other conditions, one of them being depression. PACE had also based its selection on people who were only mildly to moderately incapacitated. Since then, other research studies have gone on to determine that graded exercise is one of the least successful methods of treatment. In fact, this technique has been proven to frequently trigger a worsening of symptoms that can very often result in a relapse. SPECT scans, which analyse the functioning of different parts of the body, have uncovered that exercise substantially lowers cortisol and brain blood volume levels in people with CFS/ME (*Exercise*, n.d.).

I, along with numerous other ME sufferers and leading researchers and clinicians are astounded that these false claims are allowed to continue to permeate mainstream medicine. This method has been created and still prevails as a widely accepted form of treatment simply because of the existing stigma that regards these illnesses as psychological conditions. I can see no other explanation for its presence. This reaction can be seen in so many instances throughout history. When physical evidence for an illness has yet to be found, the medical profession is quickly inclined to assume that it must have a psychological cause, deeming the case closed. Multiple Sclerosis was generally classed as hysterical paralysis right up to the invention of the CAT scan machine in 1972 that was then able to show the patients' clearly discernible brain lesions (Brea, 2017).

I had been using pacing, the second method suggested by the

specialist centre, since I attended the three-day programme in London the year before. After being introduced to that technique, I had begun to listen to my body properly and had learned to break tasks up throughout the day. Instead of attempting to do everything all at once and then collapsing, pacing was helping me to conserve my energy, which in turn, minimised my relapses. Even though it was a useful strategy, I received no additional benefit from relearning it and unfortunately, it never helped me move beyond my baseline.

The last approach to be explained is, quite possibly, even more of a preposterous solution than the first. Cognitive behavioural therapy (CBT), a highly respected psycho-social intervention, theorises that if a person changes their thought patterns they will begin to behave differently, which will cause a positive impact on their current life situation. Offering CBT talking therapy to me as a form of treatment was based upon the same ideology that I had encountered for years; that my illness was no more than a psychological disorder. It both exasperated and saddened me deeply to hear yet another professional pass my very real and troubling medical condition off as nothing more than a mental health issue.

I refused to accept the presumption that because I had ME, I needed counselling. I gave graded exercise a chance, simply because I held hope that the service centre would be able to help me. Honestly, by now I was willing to give almost anything a go. But because of following their senseless advice, my health almost instantly took a sharp turn for the worse and the damage that ensued then took me months to recover from.

The only forms of treatment that were offered by the healthcare system from this point on were to repeat attending the specialist centre, to retry graded exercise independently (regardless of the fact that it had caused me a major setback) or to commence cognitive behavioural therapy. I felt like I was banging my head up against a brick wall.

Whenever I attended a medical appointment, I came out either depressed, crying, angry or feeling exceedingly frustrated that my illness had been, yet again, intentionally disregarded. On one occasion, after telling a doctor that I had ME, he went on to ask me: 'Besides that, are you healthy?' Can you imagine that scenario playing out on someone who has lung cancer for instance? Doctor tells patient: 'Other than the disease that is currently running rampant inside one of your vital organs, you are one remarkably healthy individual.'

This disparaging attitude was displayed, yet again, when I attempted physiotherapy in order to try and improve my ongoing rib and back pain. During my initial appointment, the specialist asked me a series of questions. They started off as ordinary movement and pain level enquiries but quickly morphed into ones about my condition. That was when the very personal and deliberate assault began to ensue.

One of the first questions routinely asked of me by practitioners was what psychological stressors had been present in my life just before I had become ill. Every time I heard that query I immediately wanted to walk out of the room as it would become apparent that the remainder of the conversation would only be going in one direction. This circumstance was no different.

The accusatory questions that were thrown at me of course began with the old favourite. The physiotherapist then went on to say, 'I can't understand, what do you feel that makes you not want to go out to work?' After learning that I used a wheelchair for assistance, she asked me in a scathing tone, 'If your house was burning down and your life was on the line are you trying to tell me that you wouldn't be able to get out in time to save yourself from the fire?' She made sure to include the comment 'You look well for someone claiming to be ill' within her speech and actually laughed at me before stating that chronic fatigue syndrome wasn't even a real illness. Her manner was completely disrespectful for the entire length of the appointment.

When I finally left the office, I broke down and cried. Not only because of *her* blatant derision but because of *all* of the accusations, underlying tones and passive aggressive comments that I had received from people over the years. I was continuously being ridiculed and disregarded, simply because of having an illness that had not shown up on any medical tests.

During my illness, I came across three separate cases of individuals who had been unfortunate enough to have experienced both ME and cancer during their lifetimes. In each of the circumstances, the person asserted that ME had been the most debilitating. The first reason given for this was the extremity of the physical symptoms they had to contend with. The level of stress involved with trying to prevent a relapse from occurring was also said to be substantially more challenging. The third causal factor reported was the mental anguish caused by the brazen disrespect people expressed to them on a daily basis. This last point was, in particular, what had made ME significantly more unfavourable.

By including these examples, my intention is in no way meant to trivialise the experience of having cancer. I have never been faced with that hardship myself and, therefore, have no idea how I would personally compare it to that of my own. The battle a person must face when struck down with that particular disease deserves the highest respect. I am simply trying to convey that ME is a horrendous condition that is worsened by the pervasive ignorance that surrounds it.

One healthcare provider extended her judgement even further when she tried to blame my illness on my mother. During a telephone appointment, the doctor declared outrightly that the reason I was unable to heal was because our mother-daughter relationship was unhealthily entwined. It is important to note that when this conclusion was formed, the woman had talked to both of us on the phone less than a handful of times. She had based most of her opinion on the fact that, after three years of attempting to cope with the responsibility of both jobs, my mum had recently given up work to become a full-time carer for me.

Instead of appreciating the necessity of this well-thought-out decision, the doctor saw the new arrangement as confirmation of my unhealthy dependency. In her eyes, I was fully capable of taking care of myself but was still asking my mum to do everything for me. To back up her unshakable theory, the GP pointed out that whenever I went to the doctor's, I took my mother into the room with me. In reality, there was a rational explanation for this behaviour. Once I became too exhausted to communicate, I would need my mum to take over for me, explaining in more detail what I would have loved to have been able to express myself. I had already told the GP this in the past but obviously it had fallen on deaf ears.

On these bases alone, my kind and loving mum was told that it was her role in our co-dependent relationship that was keeping me stuck within my current state. What right did the doctor have to make these outlandish accusations about two people she had only spoken to for no more than 20 minutes in total? To have a person that didn't know either of us, or my family history, make such judgemental comments felt completely unfair. Within the same conversation the GP also stated that, as my mother, it was her duty to help me accept that there was no other solution. As the doctor saw it, I was only wasting my energy in looking for one. I should stop searching for why I was so ill and start to focus on improving my symptoms through graded exercise and psychotherapy.

After this encounter, the disrespect that I was by now used to receiving began to feel like a very personal attack. The perpetual reaction by others that *I* was to blame for what I was going through, that *I* was cultivating my discomfort with my own thoughts, that all I needed to do to get better was to get off my backside and go back to work, was infuriating. This last experience only added fuel to the fire for me to find an answer to my terrible situation and be able to prove all of them wrong.

CHAPTER 4

THE ONLY WAY FROM HERE IS UP

I couldn't find the answer by using psychological means, nor could I find it through nutrition, and I *certainly* couldn't find it by pushing myself beyond my limits, however 'graded' it was. I realised that I was on my own in discovering what was wrong with my body and what I could do to make myself well. Whenever I came across other stories of people with ME, I found it incredible how familiar and in sync each was with my own. There were so many people out there, living every single day in the same predicament as I, who were being left with absolutely no explanation as to why. I knew that my search for the answer to this question would not be an easy one but was simultaneously aware that my illness was not something that would go away on its own. I was adamant that I would not turn into one of those people who had been living with it for over 20 years.

If I could uncover the cause of my ill health there would be much more of a chance for me to receive the correct treatment. Without this basic level of understanding over my own body the situation felt insurmountable. I had the strong gut feeling that my system was being attacked by something like a virus. My idea was supported by the fact that, initially, the illness had closely resembled the flu. In addition to this, viral malaise had remained one of my main symptoms. But this notion was just a theory. The only tangible evidence that I had ever been given was my in-depth Epstein-Barr virus test results. However, during that same appointment I had also been informed that glandular fever would not last for the length of time that I had been incapacitated for. In light of this, I considered the virus to be what had caused me to be ill in the first place but not what was keeping me trapped within my current state.

Over the years I repetitively asked my mum the same rhetorical questions; 'What is wrong with me?' 'Why is my body acting like this?' 'Why can't I live a normal life?' Every time I said these familiar words, all my mum could say in reply was that she wished she had the answers for me. She would always add that she *knew* without a shadow of a doubt that I *would* get through this. Even though I was aware that her statement was only speculation, it did give me some form of comfort. But then my questions would transform into: 'How long will it be?' 'When will I be able to live my life again?' I felt that if only there was a crystal ball with all of the answers, I could then be patient. There was a very large possibility that I would never be able to figure out why I was feeling so devastatingly ill. Every time this frightening thought entered my mind, I pushed it away. But try as I might, it kept creeping back in.

For three years I managed to stay positive and maintain that there *was* an answer out there for me. But after spending so much time putting all of my energy and faith into the London ME centre without receiving any positive results, I began to feel disheartened. I had followed everything that they instructed me to do, yet had felt no better. When I finally admitted that fact to myself, the blow was crushing. To have then entered straight into a graded exercise regime, a treatment that had brought on severe ramifications, proved too much for me to bear. I tried my hardest not to let these emerging feelings of disillusionment get the better of me but there seemed to be no way of avoiding them. The impact of what I was dealing with had finally become too much.

It was clearly impossible for the depression to have caused my symptoms as it hadn't existed until years after I had become ill. In fact, the opposite was true; the illness had caused my depression. Be that as it may, whenever I confided in anyone, more often than not, this explanation fell on deaf ears. The majority of them, especially doctors, felt vindicated in their assumptions about me. I learned very quickly not to mention my mental health, except to the few people who were willing to properly listen. My despondency lasted for about a year. During this time, I felt as though I didn't know how to keep the momentum going. I did though. I kept striving, kept researching, kept looking everywhere I could think of. I never gave up, not even for a second.

It was not only the ongoing isolation that caused my depression. There was also the fact that I had to deal with my increasingly innumerable physical symptoms every minute of the day. One of the newest additions was my developing respiratory issues. During my inbreath it had begun to feel as though I couldn't take in enough oxygen. At first, this only happened every few days for several minutes at a time. But the sensation worsened over a period of about a year until, in the end, it became a constant source of discomfort. Holding a conversation was now even more gruelling, as I could no longer take in enough air to speak a full sentence. Any small amount of physical or mental activity that I undertook caused an increase in my level of breathlessness or 'air hunger'.

Another horrible new condition to materialise was called Erythromelalgia. My feet were now ice cold all of the time except when there was any external cause for them to raise in temperature, such as taking a shower or wearing socks and shoes when I went outside. Even the tiniest adjustment would generate a very large reaction; my feet would swell up, turn bright red in colour and become boiling hot with sharp pins and needles running through them.

I had issues with body temperature regulation in general. I was often cold and found that I couldn't warm up easily and vice versa when I became too hot. I frequently woke up sweating in the middle of the night and had to peel back the covers and wait for my body to cool down, before falling back to sleep. My sleep pattern was interrupted even further when I began to wake up almost every night with the strong sensation of needing to vomit. The intense nausea lasted for a whole nine months with seemingly no rhyme or reason.

Throughout the years, I had developed a sensitivity to many household chemicals; another common symptom of ME. Coming into contact with the offensive items would cause sneezing, coughing, skin allergies and a general sense of unwellness in addition to how I already felt. All of our toiletries and cleaning products had to be as natural as possible with no artificial fragrances.

Every minute of my day was consumed by being hyperaware of how I was feeling. I had become conditioned to be on a constant lookout for any signs of my diminishing energy. I was obsessed with following the rules and regulations that I had to place upon myself in order to maintain a small amount of stamina. Control was a necessary part of my existence but was, nevertheless, extremely tedious and caused me to feel high levels of anxiety. I could never be engrossed in the moment or allow myself to do what I felt like doing, what I enjoyed doing. Every so often I would decide to act against my self-imposed rules out of sheer desperation but could never fully relax while knowing that it was only a matter of time before I would have to face the consequences.

So much of our pleasure is experienced through the senses, like when listening to music, receiving a comforting hug, looking out over a new horizon or sharing an interesting conversation. I had been deprived of this and so much more for such a long time. Being unable to enjoy the sensations of touch, sight and sound made it difficult for me to feel joy anymore. Music was one of the pastimes that I missed the most. On a few occasions I had attempted to listen to one song but after only seconds had been forced to turn it off again. In the past, listening to music had been a part of how I had connected to my emotions and a source of support when I needed to release my feelings. Now these beautiful sounds were just another form of comfort that I could no longer receive. When I look back now, I realise that it was incredible for me to have gotten as far as I did without giving in to the despair. By the time my depression set in, I had simply been starved of beauty and pleasure for far too long. It felt like this disease was slowly but surely strangling the life out of me.

I knew the importance of the role I had to play if I was to have any chance of getting out of my current reality. I began to latch on to any sort of treatment that I thought had even a modest amount of relevance or credibility. It was obvious that I could no longer turn to conventional healthcare for help. Because of this, I became quite the connoisseur of alternative medicine. There were always new ideas, new avenues, new alternative therapies to try which, quite often, felt overwhelming. I would wonder, 'Which method should I choose?' 'Will it be the right one?' 'What if I am just wasting more time, more money?' None of my prospects were clear cut as there was little if any research to back any of them up.

Whenever I commenced a new treatment, the first thing I would ask was how long it would be before I began to feel an improvement. I always received the same reply; every person is different and because of this they will react in their own way, at their own speed. I could appreciate the truth in this statement, but it didn't make the words any less frustrating for me to hear. I was eager for someone to be able to tell me the answer to my question. I hung on to any encouraging words that a practitioner ever said to me. If they indicated a three-month possibility, I would wait on tenterhooks, counting the days.

Each and every time I attempted something new, I would believe with all of my heart that that particular treatment was going to be the answer that I had been looking for. I would inevitably become let down when the suggested time frame came and went, and I hadn't noticed any development. Often, the practitioner would have to be the one to tell me that it was unlikely that my body was going to respond. Only then would I reluctantly give up. Even though each avenue I tried ended in disappointment, somehow, I would pick myself back up and dust myself off, convinced that the next treatment would be the remedy I had been looking for.

Acupuncture was one such prospective solution. During my appointments, I would lay on a bed with needles sticking out of my face, torso, and limbs, all the while praying for some relief. I gave this treatment its best shot, like I always did, only admitting defeat after the acupuncturist told me himself that he didn't believe the approach was going to work.

After discontinuing treatment with the London ME centre's nutritionist, I had tried one more practitioner based locally to me. He carried out his own tests and proceeded to recommend new supplements and diet changes. After shelling out hundreds of pounds and following every tiny instruction, it became another dead end.

Next up was something called the Bowen technique. This particular form of massage was meant to help the body to reset and heal itself. I went to three appointments but after each visit ended up feeling worse. I assume this reaction was because the therapist was using a modality that my body could not handle; touch.

To be honest, it wasn't uncommon for a new treatment to cause my health to decline. This was both very disappointing and disheartening to me. Every time I tried something new, I was aware of the gamble. I had such low energy and stamina levels to begin with that anything I attempted could easily and quickly dissolve these resources. I would then have to spend my days rebuilding my baseline before going on to explore in a new direction.

It was at around this time in my quest that I was told about a hands-on healer who had cured someone of hay fever. The successful results had taken only one session. I had participated in so many conventional methods and alternative therapies by now. However, this new technique was different from the rest as it was working purely with energy. Upon hearing the story, I became curious and thought, 'Why not give it a go myself.' Again, I went with an open mind and hope in my heart.

The specific method that the practitioner worked with was called Chirokinetic Therapy (CKT). This technique uses something called muscle testing to find imbalances within a person's energy system and determine the modifications that need to be made. The therapist then works with the cranial points to send healing to appropriate areas of the body. I travelled to see the lady approximately once a month for treatments in her home. I was told that I should make the sessions that far apart as I needed time to process the work that had been carried out. This involved releasing harmful toxins and suppressed emotions from the body.

Immediately after I had attended each appointment, my energy became depleted. I would then spend the next week laying down on the sofa, almost completely immobilised, fearing that I wasn't going to recuperate. Prior to this, whenever my body had become that drained, it had taken me months to recover. However, every time I saw this practitioner, after about a week of 'processing', my strength would somehow manage to regain itself. On top of that, I was actually able to notice small improvements.

There were many changes happening over the course of the treatment. I experienced less crashes on a day to day basis and the time it took for me to recover from each of them also reduced. Because of this I was able to participate in more light activities for longer periods of time. I was also able to stand more stimulation cognitively before the extreme headaches came on. This allowed me to share a slow conversation for 20 minutes off and on throughout the day or make an occasional short phone call. I began to take trips out in my wheelchair to quiet destinations for a couple of hours, a few times a week. My stomach had even begun to digest more foods properly again; a development I felt deeply grateful for.

Because of witnessing a gradual upwards trend in my overall health, I persisted with this particular treatment for longer than any of the others. The only problem was that, even after 12 months, I could only see marginal differences in myself. When I looked back, I realised that my health had increased no more than about 10%. Finally, reluctantly, I stopped making the once a month trip out to see the healer.

This decision was made in view of the fact that if my progression continued at the same pace as it had been, it would have taken me years to fully recover. That was substantially longer than I was willing to wait. If I had been patient with the technique, it is a possibility that I would have healed faster than I did on the actual path that I ended up taking. I can say with absolute certainty that the journey would have been far less arduous. Unfortunately, I had no awareness of this when I made my decision.

I had been ill for over four years by the time I had abandoned this latest endeavour. It was unfathomable to me that my ordeal could go on for much longer. The option that it would take more than a year at the utmost was, for me, unacceptable and, therefore, I decided that it was not going to happen.

I still lived with the subconscious belief that the world was fair. During the entirety of my extensive search I held on to the notion that I had been ill long enough. Therefore, the 'reasonable' thing was for me to get well. I am aware that my presumption had no basis in logic or reality. I was even conscious of it at the time. But nevertheless, it was how I felt. In my mind what I was searching for was always just over the next hill. It had to be. I would think, 'This is going to be the treatment that fixes me because I deserve it, because it's what is fair.'

The approach that followed came into my life in a novel way as this time it happened to find *me*. During a conversation one day, a friend of my mother's told her about another energy healer who had been featured on the Oprah show. The man had built up quite a reputation in Brazil, the country where he was based, using a modality called psychic surgery.

All of my life I had believed in the *possibility* of spontaneous healing while remaining sceptical of people who claimed that they could work wonders. I was aware of the level of risk involved in putting my hopes into a venture that had no evidence other than testimonials to back it up. If I hadn't been in the situation that I found myself in, I probably would have been curious about the prospect but taken things no further. Because of my level of desperation, I now jumped at the chance to go. There was no consideration of how taxing the journey would be on my body, no thoughts about what had happened to me the last time I had made a gigantic trip. My focus remained solely on the fact that I had been presented with another chance to be well. At this point I was willing to give anything a go.

My mum booked the tickets for us both. I had no idea how I was going to make it from England to Brazil, but I didn't care. None of it mattered because I now had something new to try, a new form of hope. Being given a fresh opportunity felt more gratifying to me than continuing to struggle to find something proven and substantial. It kept me fired up and gave me a reason to keep putting one foot in front of the other. If I had been left without a way to work towards my healing, I don't think I could have kept going.

I made the journey with my mum in tow, neither of us having any idea of what to expect. During the flight my body was slumped in the chair and remained in a constant state of high distress. All I could do was moan and wish the hours away until I would feel some relief. The utter desperation to find an answer was the only thing that gave me the extra adrenaline that coursed through my veins and the strength of character needed to make it through the entire flight. As soon as we arrived at our accommodation I collapsed into bed and lay in agony. However, in that moment the pain hardly mattered to me. I was simply relieved to be in a place that provided me with another chance to be whole again. I waited with a sense of renewed hope.

The healing centre was a simple building that consisted of a large open hall with another room attached to the rear. This was where individuals went when it was their turn to visit the healer. It was surrounded by a beautiful and tranquil garden that contained devoted areas for people to sit and meditate together whenever they wanted to. There were many volunteers walking around the premises wearing white clothing. They were there to assist everyone, cook the soup that was provided at lunchtime and take care of the halls. The main energy healing was provided for free and any additional treatments were offered at a very reasonable cost.

On the day that it was my turn, I sat in my wheelchair and waited in the hall along with hundreds of other people. When it was time, I, amongst a small group of other hopefuls, entered the back room in silence. The healer came in not long afterwards and said something in Portuguese. After that, a translator told us to close our eyes. This signified the moment when the psychic surgery would begin. It was not real surgery. No one came near me during the time that I was in the room. The healing was provided instead, through the passing of energy.

At this point in my story I may lose the respect of many of my readers. Some of you will think me ridiculous, you may laugh at me, you may think that I am gullible or even stupid. All I can say in answer to this is that if you were in my position, if you were *this* desperate, you might surprise yourself as to what you would try. You might be much more willing to open your heart and mind to something if there was even a small chance that it would give you precisely what you had spent so many years in frantic pursuit of. While waiting in that room, I did just that; I opened my heart to this wildly alternative form of treatment.

Immediately after receiving the 'surgery' we were instructed to go back to our rooms and rest in bed for 24 hours. In addition to this, capsules of herbs were given to us to take orally for the next three months. We were told that the results we hoped for would come within that time period. When I returned to my hotel room, I felt the same energy sapping effect that any new treatment seemed to have on me, except to a much higher degree. In fact, I had never experienced a setback of this magnitude before. I was unable to leave my bed as all of my symptoms, including my viral malaise, had been acutely amplified. On top of that I had a fever, diarrhoea, and a sharp intermittent pain in my ears. However, after five days had passed I was finally able to get up, and when I did, I felt a vast improvement. On my first day out of bed, I decided to test my body and see how far it could move. My target was to walk to a shop that was around the corner from where we were staying. I went at a snail's pace, and had to take a rest halfway, but nevertheless, I made it there. Upon this accomplishment I felt like a new person. I was thrilled to be able to walk for five whole minutes without the use of a wheelchair. It seemed as though what I had been yearning for had finally begun to happen. After three days of observing that these positive changes were remaining stable, I made the momentous decision to donate my wheelchair to the centre. I felt that the deed was necessary in order for me to put my whole heart into the process that was taking place.

Many of you will assume that it must have been the power of the mind that caused my increase in energy and stamina. You may give other excuses for this transformation. I would never propose to know for sure what it was that transpired during that trip. But what actually happened doesn't really matter. Something had changed in me and I was ecstatic about it.

This new energy continued to pervade my body until I returned home several days later. The flight back was difficult, but I didn't feel even half the amount of discomfort I had experienced on the way over. I did feel terribly drained, but there was no way that coping in that manner would have been remotely possible before this point. When my dad picked us up, I came out to the arrivals lounge with a huge smile on my face and was even able to hug him hello from the airport wheelchair. He couldn't believe it. To see me this way after a 12-hour flight was astounding to him.

Unfortunately, when he arrived at the airport my dad had the flu, and all of the fairness in the world couldn't have stopped me from catching it. Three days after I got home, I became very ill. I was then stuck in bed for a further two weeks while the virus attacked my body. After it had passed, I found that I had reverted right back to my old baseline. It was as if I had never even been to Brazil.

I kept longing for the changes I had witnessed to return, believing that it was just a matter of time before I would pick up strength again. But sadly, my expectations never came to fruition. Having the substantial upwards shift taken away from me as quickly as it had come was quite a blow to my spirits. I began ruminating; 'Why did I have to catch that flu? Why did my dad have to be ill in the first place? Why couldn't I have had more time to conserve my strength?' I didn't understand why the world had to work that way. It felt as though the universe was conspiring against me. The fact was that this was how events had played out and there was no way of changing them. Not long after returning home we invested in another wheelchair.

I started to become tired of hearing new ideas, of listening to all of the well-intentioned people I knew suggesting yet another avenue to go down; something they had found on the internet, something a friend had told them about or something they had seen on TV. I also felt jaded by all of the statements I read online: 'Try my treatment.' 'Spend your money.' 'Listen to us.' 'We know what we're talking about, we can make you well.' 'Do something from the medical system that's been tried and tested.' 'Do something new that is fresh and innovative.' 'Do something spiritual, something helping the psyche, something strengthening the immune system, something nutritional.'

There was always another new strategy professing that it was the answer. Every one that I came across claimed to provide the quintessential panacea. They made sure to make it clear to their customer that no one else knew the solution but them. I became fed up with hearing it.

All of the recommendations shared by friends and family came from a place of love and, because of this, I was appreciative of each and every one of them. However, once I became aware of a new approach it would create tremendous anxiety for me as I worried that the proposition in question could be the one that *would* work.

That meant that if I decided not to participate in it, I would be missing out on the only thing that had a chance to make me well and I would then remain ill forever. I felt terrified of passing anything up and yet sick to death of trying and failing. I am not saying that I wanted to stop. Nonetheless, when I initially heard the new proposal I felt the need to heave a giant sigh as if to say, 'Here we go again.'

Three months had passed since I returned home from Brazil and I still hadn't moved beyond my baseline. Once I had recovered from the consequences of having the flu and after giving it a short amount of consideration, I decided to go back to the same location. My reasoning was, 'If it worked the first time, why wouldn't it work the second?' I made the trip on my own this time as my mum had hurt her back and was unable to fly. I realised that there was a possibility that I would not be able to cope with the challenge of it all but again, I didn't care. I was all too aware that my chances of finding a cure were dwindling.

Sadly, the travelling alone proved too much for my body to sustain such a short time after the last trip I had made. After arriving to my room, I could manage no more than to lay in bed for the rest of the day. This level of debilitation persisted for the entirety of my stay. Out of necessity, meals were taken to me in bed and everything was cleaned and washed by some kind participants of the healing centre. Because of the severe state I was now in, even the smallest acts were taking their toll on me. This included washing and dressing myself, sitting upright while waiting my turn for the surgery, and, most of all, having to voice all of my many needs to the people who were helping me throughout the day. If my mother had been there, she would have carried out these tasks without having to be instructed. I was aware of the effect each individual exertion was having on me. Be that as it may, I was alone, far away from home, with no other choice than to do what was necessary for me to receive the healing that I had come for.

When the time came for me to go to the centre, I was taken the short distance by taxi. A kind stranger then wheeled me from there to the room where the healer was waiting. Immediately after being given my second psychic surgery I collapsed and was rushed to bed. What followed was the worst repercussion I had ever experienced during the four and a half years that I had been ill.

My energy became so low that, from then on, I could barely make it to the toilet, even though it was a mere few steps away. By the end of each day my resources had been completely consumed just from getting to the bathroom and back. My body would then spend the entire night as I slept trying to recover. Meals continued to be brought to me in bed. However, now the plate had to be rested on my stomach as I no longer had the strength to sit up. Even the act of bringing the fork to my mouth severely drained me. I would take a bite of food every couple of minutes but could hardly manage to make the movements that were required to eat one mouthful. In order to accomplish this, I would chew once and then stop for about 30 seconds, then chew again and stop and so on, until the food was ready to swallow.

If you have never experienced a level of depletion of this intensity before, it will be impossible for you to comprehend. No description that I could provide would enable you to fully grasp the lethargy that I felt. On top of that, I was experiencing mind-blowing headaches, difficulties with my breathing and severe viral malaise. While lying completely still, I now lived in a state of pure agony. If I expended any energy at all, however small, a wave of exhaustion would come over me so unbearable that I didn't know how I was going to endure it for one more second.

I was alone, trapped and panic-stricken. I had no idea how I was going to fly half the way across the world if I couldn't even get out of bed to get my own food. But my return home was unavoidable. Without my mum there to take care of me there was no way that I could begin to regain my strength again. It was very frightening for me to watch my health deteriorating so rapidly. We were also running out of money to pay for my inordinate stay.

I still, to this day, don't know how I managed it. Someone packed my bags. Another person helped me to lay down in the taxi that took me to the airport. When I got there, I was wheeled into a special room where I could lay down on my own until I boarded the plane. The journey kept on in that fashion until I made it home. I had planned on staying in Brazil for two weeks. In the end, I was there for six.

My body had sustained such extreme devastation. So much so, that when I came home, I went to bed and was unable to leave it again. After a few weeks I could chew my food properly and feed myself without suffering serious consequences. I was also able to watch TV or read for about fifteen minutes twice a day and could have approximately two ten-minute conversations from my bed. During these times, my mum would come into my room in order to break up the monotony but what was said had to be kept slow and quiet. Even though it felt wonderful to have some company, I would end up regretting the visit each time as it consumed so much of my energy. Regardless of this, the next day I would repeat the process all over again.

All my symptoms had heightened substantially. It was like having the worst flu you can imagine day after day with no end in sight. My bedroom had to be kept completely quiet all of the time. The only period that I left it was when I washed myself and even that task I now needed assistance with. I had a commode positioned right next to where I lay. It was a struggle to get in and out of bed each time I had to use it, but I still managed to do that on my own, thank goodness. I wore a nightshirt 24 hours a day as I didn't have the energy it took to change my clothes. My mum began to cut up the food that she gave me as I could no longer use a knife. Everything that was even remotely strenuous had to be taken care of for me.

It was during this period that both of my elbow joints started to become exceedingly painful in the night. I wasn't sure why this was happening but thought that I possibly had a condition such as rheumatism. When the ache woke me up from my sleep the only thing that I could do to alleviate the feeling was to slowly bend the afflicted joints. After a couple of minutes the pain would gradually subside. Around the same time, both hip joints also began to cause me serious discomfort, although this dull pain couldn't compare to the sharpness and severity of what I was experiencing in my arms. In this case I assumed it must have been from all of the pressure that my joints were enduring while laying on them continuously.

In recent months, my issues with breathing had become one of the hardest things for me to contend with. They had worsened so drastically that I now felt a tremendous amount of air hunger all of the time. When I attempted to speak, I would have to stop after every two or three words and take in a big breath in order to be able to push out the rest of what I wanted to say. My breathing would become so shallow during the night that I would repeatedly wake up with an urgent need to gasp for air. It would have been wonderful if I could have slept the hours away in order to escape from my reality, but my brain was still constantly racing. I felt exhausted from the lack of sleep even though I was in no way drowsy.

My stomach issues had been exacerbated so that I was experiencing diarrhoea on a regular basis again. For a few days after each bout I could only tolerate plain chicken and white rice until my belly settled. Because of the inadequacy of my diet I would then become constipated for days on end. On and on this laboursome cycle went. I felt weak from not being able to digest enough food, both in amount and nutrition, while simultaneously struggling with extreme hypoglycaemia. However, nothing I ate seemed to quench my hunger and feelings of wooziness.

The sensitivities to sound, sight and touch that I had always dealt with in the past had now become exceptional. My room had to be kept dim at all times as bright light would completely overwhelm me. I no longer had any form of touch as it was simply not worth the immediate and horrible aftermath. It was imperative that my surroundings remained quiet except for the handful of times a day when I could have a slow, gentle conversation or watch some TV. However, my brain was unable to compute the new information within the normal speed at which the shows were played out. Each time I attempted to watch anything, I would be left feeling utterly confused by what I had just seen.

I wasn't even able to have the windows open anymore. The energy it took for my body to adjust to the temperature change, breathe in the fresh air and hear the birds singing had become all too demanding; another sure sign to my NHS doctors that I was 'opting out of life'. Within the first year of being bedridden there were two or three instances in which I ventured outside, simply because of how desperate I felt. Each time, I would sit down against a wall of our house, inhaling the fresh air. It felt so healthy and clean, as if my lungs were rejuvenating with each breath that I took. But within a few minutes I lamented ever having gone outside and that regret would last for the entirety of the week that my body took to recover. My 30th birthday passed me by while I was still confined to my bed. In order to commemorate the occasion, my incredibly thoughtful mother had arranged for all of my close friends and family members to send Chinese lanterns into the sky on the eve of my birthday along with their personal healing wishes for me. I was emailed videos of each of them to watch little by little throughout the day. That gift felt so meaningful at a time when there was nothing left for anyone to offer but the love, hope and prayers that they all had for me.

Turning thirty was a major age landmark, one that honed in on the passing of time. It made it unavoidable for me to notice just how long I had been ill. The day was also quite symbolic for me. This was owing to the fact that a couple of years into my illness, after I had become aware that I was in for the long haul, I had asserted, 'There is *no* way I will still be ill by the time I am thirty.' The number had represented a cut-off point. In my mind, it had been completely unreasonable and therefore impossible for my fate to remain unchanged by the time I reached that age. Finding myself still laying in my bed meant that this inconceivability had become a devastating reality. That realisation caused a profound fear in me and, for the first time, left me genuinely wondering if I would ever be well again.

Not long afterwards, during a visit with my mum, a relative had popped into my room for a minute to say hello. As she was leaving, she said, 'The only way from here is up.' At that time, I didn't believe that anything could be more torturous than what I had experienced in Brazil. Little did I know, the darkness that lay before me would be far more harrowing than I could have ever imagined.

Graduation from master's degree Program - 2007

Ziplining in Costa Rica, just before I became ill.

Part of an average day: Enjoying a moment in which I was able to sit up and read a page in my book.

Rare moments of connection.

Out in the fresh air (one of those lucky days).

CHAPTER 5

TIME FLIES WHEN YOU'RE HAVING FUN

I spent the better part of a year in this sorry state, impatiently waiting for something else to come along. A more fitting phrase would be the 'worst' part of a year.

I had watched my health deteriorate over time. Everything I had tried had ended in failure. Despite all that had happened and how ghastly my situation had become, I remained undeterred. I held on to my deeply rooted faith that something would come to save me. I *would* find what I had been desperately searching for all these years. As I lay there in the silence, I could not fathom why this confidence was still a part of me.

Saying that I knew I would be well is oversimplifying things a little. It was like an instinctual knowledge in the background of my thoughts. It existed in the very core of my being. Was it no more than a protection mechanism, put in place so that I could somewhat ignore the possibility that there was nothing out there for me? Or perhaps it was an innate drive within to keep believing and trying and pushing, because if I stopped, if I had no hope, I wouldn't have survived. I often felt frightened as my logical mind repeatedly questioned my intuition. But the fear was on the surface. Underneath that fear was the urge to make things change.

Because of lying in that bed day after day, with nowhere else to go but inside my own head, I began to over analyse everything. After all the years I had spent listening to others' countless judgements, doctors' especially, I started to have moments in which I would wonder if they could be right. In the past, there was no way I would have even considered it. But after so many years of having these messages drilled into me, my doubts had finally begun to sneak in. The questions, 'What if I *am* causing this? What if it's all in my head?' began to creep into my mind now and then. These occasions of uncertainty were very alarming. They made me feel fragile, confused and doubtful of myself and all that I had known to be true.

Each time these self-defeating thoughts arose, I would find the strength to push them aside. In substitution, I would remind myself of the evidence: I had experienced extreme physical symptoms every day for over five years, the flu-like symptoms had come on suddenly, my previous medical history included no unexplained illnesses or psychiatric concerns and at the onset of the illness I had been a happy, balanced individual. In view of this extensive proof, it seemed significantly more plausible that doctors simply had not yet found the cause of my very real physical complaint. Although I realised having a physician admit to this was not likely to happen any time soon, I would not cower down and submit, no matter what. I knew that I had to get out of my bed, I had to get better and because of this I would become determined once again.

Any and all energy I had was now put into coming up with a new plan of action. I focused all of my attention on this for as long and as hard as I could without putting myself into risk of a further relapse. My mum took over the research aspect for me since my body was too debilitated to do it myself. Any prospect that I thought of would be passed over for her to look into further. My new objective became to contact top doctors within the field of ME treatment and research. The search began in England, but my mum looked as far as the United States and Canada. The only ones allowed on the list were those that respected the illness and considered it a real and serious condition.

My mum ended up with a handful of names to find contact information for. After doing this, she then began to call each of them in no particular order. Most of the doctors were doing research studies on potential treatments. I thought that it might be possible to become a guinea pig in one of their clinical trials. If not, they could at least lead me in the right direction of where to go next. It turned out that no one could help us. They said that I was too ill to take part in their studies since I was unable to even leave my bed in order to reach them. Not one of them had any idea of where to refer me to as, they explained, they were research doctors only and did not actually treat people with the disease.

I decided to switch tactics. I had my mum look for any and all names that had an actual standing in the world of ME. One of these was a highly respected activist and professor who had spent years trying to convince the medical system that the illness was in fact real. Over the decades he had put in an immense amount of effort fighting on behalf of people with the condition. When my mum got in contact with the man, he kindly agreed to speaking with her over the phone and, upon hearing my story, expressed a deep level of kindness and sympathy for the position we found ourselves in. Although saddened, he was not at all surprised about the insufferable treatment I had received from the many healthcare professionals I had come into contact with over the years.

As my mum went through my medical history, the professor listened carefully to all she had to say. After she shared the results of my EBV tests, he told her it was highly probable that the virus was the cause of my current state of debilitation. He had personally never heard of anyone with as high scores as I had. This was the test that had been given to me only nine months into my illness. The answer that I had been looking for had been right in front of me all along but up until now, I had never been made aware of it. After all of these years, the professor was the first person to have explained to us that the results were both seriously abnormal and greatly significant. He then proceeded to inform my mum that there was actually a treatment for the virus. In one phone call I had been given both the answer to why I had been so ill and, even more remarkably, how I could resolve it. The man explained that the medicine, an antiviral drug, was very new and therefore, still in research stages. Clinical trials had properly begun the same year that I became ill. The substance was working for people like me; the ones who had a flu like onset and persistent dysfunction of the central nervous system. There were two doctors that were supplying the treatment in America; one in California and the other in Michigan. He provided us with their names and told my mum to contact them right away.

Upon hearing the professor's words, I burst into tears. I was elated over all of the miraculous news that I had just been given. I also felt extremely grateful for him taking the time to listen to my story while giving the illness his full regard. His unbiased treatment of my case was a revelation to me. All I had known up until this point was for doctors to immediately pass me off as having a mental health condition, certainly never having an interest in my medical history (unless you included asking me what stressors I had been contending with directly preceding the onset of my symptoms). I had just been informed that a solution was actually out there after all of the years that I had been searching. The fact that I had test results that proved that something was physically wrong with me was almost more pleasurable than knowing that I could receive treatment for it. But not quite.

I felt such anger towards all of the doctors that I had come into contact with up until now. I had possessed blood test results confirming the reason for my ill health since not even a year into my illness. If they had been recognised during that early stage, I could have been treated for the Epstein-Barr virus and then been able to resume a normal life. Instead I had been left to suffer needlessly for all of these years. If I had been afforded with the knowledge of what had been causing my symptoms all along, I never would have had to endure the endless disparaging remarks from others, alongside all of the mental pain and anguish that I had experienced because of them. I would have been able to tell all of those doctors, nurses, strangers and well-intentioned friends and family members that I had a real, quantifiable illness. If they disagreed with me on this, I could have told them to bugger off.

The next obstacle that I faced was to figure out how I was going to receive the treatment. The fact that the closest destination was a nine-hour flight away made it a little tricky. My PoTS symptoms had been affected quite substantially after the second trip to Brazil. My blood pressure now fell dramatically as soon as I sat up or stood. I had to race to accomplish the few tasks that I could still do, such as eating or going to the toilet, so that I could immediately lay down again. When in an upright position, it felt as though my whole body was shutting down and it would scream at me to lay flat. This terrible aftermath always took me a long time to recover from. In light of this, we had no idea of how to proceed but decided to phone both of the doctors anyway in order to find out more information.

The University in California had a five-year waiting list. Yes, you read that right. So many other desperate individuals like myself had already signed up for the same research study. Upon hearing this, it hit home just how prevalent my condition was and how many people were left alone, with seemingly no way out. I opted to put my name down on the list anyway as I was aware of the possibility that I could still be laying in my bed when that moment came. It was a horrible thought but one that I was unable to rule out.

After being informed of this lengthy wait time, I prayed that the other location would be the answer. When my mum made the phone call, she discovered that this one was an actual doctor's office. The physician saw his patients and prescribed the medication to them from there. The receptionist informed her that the antiviral drug fought a handful of different viruses including Epstein-Barr. It was a long-term treatment but was having very high success rates. My mum was told that I could become a patient with them and begin receiving the drug right away.

On the one hand this news was the best that I had been given in all of the five years that I had been ill. On the other, how was I going to get to Michigan? Because of the lengthy treatment process, we were going to have to move there. This would take time and planning on my mum's behalf. We had five pets between us to consider, an entire household of furniture, a car to sell, the list went on and on. It would cost the earth to move. How were we going to fund all of this, let alone the actual medication? How was my mum going to be able to travel ahead without me, find a place to live and make it habitable if she was needed right here by my side 24/7? We thought and thought. After racking our brains as to how we could accomplish it all, we eventually came to the conclusion that it simply wasn't viable.

Being the determined and headstrong person that I am, I had always done whatever was required of me in my aim to be well, no matter the risk involved. Michigan seemed like it was the only real hope I had left. I was sure that I would rather risk my life than waste away in the hell that I now found myself in. However, I also knew that if I had managed to live through the journey, which was highly unlikely at this stage, I would be left too ill for the medication to have any real chance of helping me.

On top of my feelings of uncertainty, my mum was also very worried. Being aware of my precariously poor health, she knew that she had to come up with another way. We let go of Michigan for the moment and instead began to research if there was anywhere in England that supplied the same antiviral treatment. Astonishingly, there *was* somewhere to be found. The place was a day clinic located just outside of London. After hearing this news, I became full of excitement and hope; The mountain I had to climb ceased to appear insurmountable. Being well had now become an actual possibility instead of a dream.

The clinic was incredible; treating ME, sensitivities, allergies, and lots of other illnesses in which people had been left alone by the medical system. They specialised in conditions like mine where, after routine tests came back negative, patients were told that they were going to have to live with their symptoms. The owner of the day clinic took these seemingly hopeless cases on and would not give up on them. Neither would she accept any previous prognoses of ME or chronic fatigue syndrome as final. Instead, she was determined to find the true cause of why these people were ill in an attempt to help them make a full recovery. In order to accomplish this, she carried out many alternative tests on her clients including nutritional analyses, food and chemical sensitivity panels, heavy metal tests, and viral panels. Because of this extensiveness, in many cases she was successful in discerning the crucial information that conventional medicine could not find.

Not unexpectedly, this level of devotion came at a price; a very large price. We had found the answer but did not have the funds to make it into a reality. That was when four extraordinarily generous members of my family stepped in and told us that they would pay for my treatment. My aunts and uncles decided that they would split the cost between them. We were told that whatever I needed they would provide, no expense spared. This endeavour was going to be very long and very thorough and yet they remained unfazed. Their level of altruism provided me with the biggest chance to get well that I had ever been given. I was fortunate to have family members that were as affluent as they were benevolent, something that cannot be said for many others in my position.

The clinic was the only one of its kind in England and yet there are thousands of people that have been left to live with their undiagnosed conditions. This made for a very long waiting list. It took five whole months for me to become a patient. In the meantime, I was given a thorough questionnaire asking me about my symptoms and history. All of my cognitive disturbances had become much more pronounced so that it was now very difficult for me to concentrate or think. If I tried to comprehend anything it would consume all of my waning energy and cause the always agonising, pressure inducing headaches to come on. In my weakened state, the profusion of pages took me a very long time to fill out. Thankfully, I had plenty of it.

Before being admitted, I was also requested to provide my medical records from the NHS. When reading through them my mum discovered a shocking piece of information; the first time I had been referred to a CFS/ME service centre while staying with my father, I had been rejected. The consultant physician and specialist had seen my EBV antibody levels and decided that I needed, instead, to be referred to either an infectious diseases consultant or an immunologist. He had then written a detailed letter stating that my results indicated an underlying infectious disease or immune-suppressed condition. Attached to this was information about the same exact doctor that we had recently located in Michigan, including details about the same antiviral drug I had been trying to get my hands on. This correspondence had been sent out to me after I had been ill for only ten months.

After reading the page, my mum and I were both completely dismayed by all of the years that had been wasted, all of the pain and misery that I had been through for nothing. If I had seen that letter when it had been sent, all of my problems could have been resolved so easily. At that time I was physically stronger and living in America. Therefore, it would have been so much easier for me to make the required trip in order to receive the treatment. Why had it not been discovered before now? Somehow, we had to let this go and move forward. I was finally on the path that was intended for me all of those years ago.

As I was in no way able to make it to the clinic myself, when I finally became a patient, a doctor travelled the hour and a half that it took to visit me in my bed. He gave me a physical examination whilst respecting my need for silence and gentle touch. He took my extensive medical history from my mother, never making one comment about her speaking to him on my behalf. The infamous question regarding my mental health during onset never once came up. The man deemed my condition a real illness and spoke about it with the respect that it deserved.

Blood was drawn from me while I was laying in my bed. The tests to be carried out included the same EBV antibodies test that I had been given nine months after my illness first began plus many other viruses that had never been considered before. It was through testing me this thoroughly using only highly respected laboratories, alongside my detailed medical assessment form and physical examination, that my new doctor unearthed the real answer to what had been happening to me. After almost six years of living with a severe illness, she was the first healthcare professional to give me an official medical diagnosis. It turned out that I had Lyme disease.

I had been tested for the infection once before. However, the basic test that is available on the NHS has a low sensitivity meaning that it has a low success rate of detecting the illness when it is present in the body. Another problem is that it only looks for a limited number of strains of the disease. Both of these issues make it possible for a person to receive a negative result when it is in fact positive; a widely known fact shared amongst specialist Lyme disease doctors. Of course, I had no way of knowing that when my test was carried out about two years into my illness. At that time, I had full faith in the medical system and blood testing. I wasn't aware that it was possible for a test result to provide a false negative. I simply read the seemingly evident result and thought no more of it.

High-quality tests do exist but of course they come at a price. It is clearly a false economy for the government to provide substandard testing when Lyme has been suspected. If a person is fortunate enough to be diagnosed early on, a two to three-week course of oral antibiotics is usually sufficient to resolve the infection. However, without detection, that same person is likely to cost the country thousands of pounds through their ever-mounting medical needs over the years that they remain ill.

No other person had thought of rechecking me for the disease until now. In order for it to be detected, my blood had been sent to a handful of well-respected laboratories in both the United States and

Germany. The most highly recommended test, the Western blot, had been included within the array of ones that were given. The results came back positive. This test has a high specificity which means that when using it there is rarely a false positive made. Another respected form of test called a MELISA was also carried out to provide further confirmation. It has an even higher specificity of 97% meaning that only 3% of all positive results are false positives. It returned conclusive of the presence of the disease.

I also had many other simultaneous infections present in my bloodstream. This is a common occurrence with Lyme as dormant pathogens can be reactivated that have been contracted at various points in a person's life. My body had been fighting so many things at once, not only the devastating effects of Lyme disease but also six other co-infections. They were all partially responsible for lowering my immune system and stamina even more. One of these was EBV, which when tested for again, produced the same off the chart results. My physician, who had been working with exceptional cases like mine for decades, told my mum that the findings of this specific test were some of the most remarkable she had ever seen.

Of course, there was no way in hell that the graded exercise and psychotherapy that the NHS was so keen to dispense was ever going to have been able to help me. Neither was going for a run or getting a job, as many people had insinuated. For the first time I understood exactly why using acupuncture, supplements or any of the other alternative treatments I had tried had never worked.

After all of the years I had spent fighting for medical professionals to listen to me and respect that I had an illness, for all of the years of doubt and fear and wondering why I looked so normal and yet felt so ill inside, why I could not get back into the world but instead became progressively worse, I FINALLY had an answer to it ALL. It had been irrevocably confirmed that I had a seriously debilitating illness and without proper treatment I would not get better. It did not matter what anyone said, from now on I would always have this knowledge. To me, that was worth its weight in gold.

Since the beginning, I had felt deep in my heart that if I had been given the right tests, something would be found. I had a strong instinct that my body was being attacked by some form of pathogen. It turns out that my feelings were right. If only doctors could have agreed to look further. When the magnitude of wide-ranging tests had been ordered it felt incredible, even before I had received the results, as I had finally been given the attention that I deserved. All of my reported symptoms had been regarded as medical concerns instead of disregarded as signs of depression, anxiety or any other mental illness. In short, this doctor had listened. We could hear it in her responses. Everything my mum told her was noted down and considered to be a piece of the puzzle, no matter how small it seemed. It was such a breath of fresh air after spending almost six years feeling as though I had been drowning underwater.

Based upon my medical history, presenting symptoms and examination, my self-diagnosis of ME was also confirmed. You might be wondering why my doctor decided to include it in my records when the pathogens responsible for my infirmity had been clearly defined. ME is a name for a set of symptoms, those of which I still had. The Lyme had manifested itself within those parameters from the very beginning. I firmly believe that *everyone* with ME has a real illness with a real cause. A tangible reason for my symptoms had finally been discovered because I had found a physician who knew the gravity of that statement and would not stop looking until she had procured an answer.

It is feasible to suggest that Lyme disease is responsible for what is plaguing a great number of people who currently have a diagnosis of CFS or ME. Until adequate testing is routinely provided for the multitude of existing sufferers we will never know. Thank god for this clinic and the ground-breaking steps that they are taking in order to help people like me.

My mum began to research my newly discovered condition. She would then give me a short synopsis of the information to read every day so that I could learn about it for myself. Lyme disease is a bacterial infection that is spread through the bite of a tick. The pathogen begins by resembling the flu and is able to attack any organ, causing a wide range of symptoms. A tell-tale sign of transmission is if a person develops a bullseye rash around the area of the bite. Although this is an easy way to detect the transference, it does not necessarily have to be a symptom. It is possible to have a different style of rash or none at all (Lymedisease.org, 2017). I had never seen a bullseye pattern on my body but a red rash had appeared on my back when I first became ill.

If detected early on, treatment for Lyme disease should be a fairly quick and straightforward process. An early diagnosis is of paramount importance as the longer it remains in the body untreated, the less chance a person has of recovering. Once the disease becomes chronic, symptoms grow ever more severe and treatment is a much more complicated and drawn out process with dwindling success rates (Lymedisease.org, 2017).

At present, awareness about Lyme disease is very limited. Because of doctors' lack of knowledge surrounding its multi-bodily system symptoms, in addition to the inadequate forms of testing that are administered, sufferers are frequently misdiagnosed with CFS/ME, psychiatric disorders, and MS. This insufficient level of response is allowing the disease to persist, undetected. People all over the world are left to suffer the consequences of this widespread ignorance within the medical system.

It is a sad state of affairs that currently many highly respected medical bodies including the NHS do not recognise that chronic Lyme disease even exists. I don't exactly know what they imagine happens to the bacteria if left untreated. Maybe it goes up in smoke, or the Lyme fairies come and take it away. In any case, it becomes exceedingly difficult to attain antibiotics after a certain amount of time has passed. Another reason for this is that the general standpoint amongst doctors, private ones included, is that antibiotics have a poor prognosis after the disease has progressed past the early stages. Therefore, even many of the doctors who believe in chronic

Lyme's existence will be reluctant to administer the much-needed drugs. In the meantime, countless lives are currently being ruined by the condition's devastating effects.

My new physician was not willing to follow these traditional assumptions blindly. She belonged to the small minority of innovative thinkers within the medical field who both believed in and treated chronic Lyme infection. By the time I had become a patient at her clinic, she had been successfully treating people for decades. Because of the extensive lack of knowledge, many a person had come through her doors with a pre-existing diagnosis of MS and left cured after being treated for Lyme disease.

Due to the highly progressive nature of this work, the clinic was afforded no respect from conventional medical bodies. The healthcare system was constantly trying to put a stop to the doctor's endeavours despite the fact that she was helping so many people that would have otherwise had no hope. We received personal confirmation of this success in the coming months as my mum spoke with no end of patients who shared their individual stories of progress with her. She also met many ex-patients on their revisit to the clinic. They would come for no other reason than to say thank you; for believing in them, for testing them and for treating them properly for their conditions.

It is greatly upsetting to me that this pervasive ignorance exists, yet it has been the same story throughout all of history. As human beings, we seem to find it very difficult to adopt a new concept if it means that, in doing so, we must let go of our pre-established belief systems. Many people are reluctant to take a chance on some new idea or recognise and acknowledge the signs when an innovative method is proving effective.

Because of how ill I had become, my practitioner informed us that I would need to receive treatment in the day clinic during all of the hours that it was open; 9 am until 5 pm, six days a week. I couldn't even leave my bed, let alone travel the hour and a half it took to get to the outskirts of London every day. Therefore, it was essential that we moved locally. Without hesitation, my mum took care of all of the arrangements to make this possible whilst continuing to provide around the clock care for me. She would have moved mountains if it could have provided me with even a small chance of getting well.

It was while planning the move, that we both came to the sad realisation that our pets could not come with us. For the last few years, I had been feeling guilty over the level of care that I was able to personally deliver to them but had never before considered giving away members of my family. In my mind I was always one step away from finding my cure and would soon be able to resume my responsibilities. Now that we had found the day clinic, I presumed that it would be no more than six months at most before I was strong enough to travel back and forth for my treatment. My father and his wife selflessly agreed to live in our house to take care of our pets for that length of time. My immediate family was coming together to do whatever was necessary now.

Because of being confined to one room at all times, moving wouldn't be much of a change for me. I was simply exchanging one small space for another. It was harder on my mother, but it helped her to think that we would be able to return home within a six-month period. She found a place for us to live that was right around the corner from the clinic and took only two minutes to drive to in the car.

An ambulance took me to our new home in case my health took a turn for the worse during the long journey. Unfortunately for me, that ride was made during the middle of a heatwave. To make matters even worse, we got stuck in a major traffic jam. Because of this, our intended one and a half hour trip ended up taking two and a half hours in total. With no air conditioning or windows to open, I lay in the back of the ambulance, getting hotter and weaker by the minute, silently panicking if I would ever recover. By the time I reached the flat, the length of the journey and the suffocating heat had finished me off. I was rushed up in the lift, slouching as low as I could in a wheelchair as by this point I could not sit up. I made it to my new room and was put into bed, but it was too late, the damage had already been done.

Before starting at the day clinic, I was afforded a few days of rest. I was more eager than ever for my treatment to commence as I had never felt such a level of depletion as I did now. My entire existence had become one prolonged crash, identical to the sensation I used to experience temporarily after partaking in far too strenuous an activity. During each of those murderous times when I had pushed my body and mind way past their limits, I would close myself off to the world and wait in desperation until the extreme suffering had finally subsided. The only way I had survived each of these ordeals was to concentrate on the fact that the severity of my symptoms was temporary and would soon fade. Without the promise of any alleviation, there was now nowhere I could put my mind in order to try to escape from the crippling torment that defined every moment. Can you remember a time when you stubbed your toe, really gave it a good whack? We've all done it. You cry out, grab a hold of it, hop around the room and possibly even fall to the floor in agony while waiting for the throbbing to subside. Now imagine if that pain never diminished, not even a little bit. How would you manage? The level of suffering that I now had no choice but to sustain was, I can assure you, significantly worse than a stubbed toe. The debilitation that I had experienced in that ambulance had been so substantial that my body simply could not recuperate. I wouldn't wish the torture I was grappling with on anybody, not even all of those ignorant doctors that I had come into contact with over the years. Well, maybe for a *little* while, just enough time for them to gain a bit of empathy.

From this point forward, I could no longer speak at all. Neither could I be spoken to. Hearing any utterance would cause all my symptoms to become so incredibly excruciating that it felt like I was going to die, no exaggeration. I would save up a small list of approximately three to five words to say in succession at the end of each day to express my immediate needs. They would take me less than a minute to go through as quickly as I could. This was all I was capable of doing as even then my energy would plummet and my head would feel like it was going to explode. My mum became very astute at reading their meanings. If I needed an extra blanket, once the day came to an end I would say 'cold' or if a certain food I ate had caused me a stomach upset I would say 'carrot bad' for example. 'Loud' was another word commonly repeated alongside whatever small noise I had been able to hear.

I would spend time trying to figure out the best combination of words to use in order to get my point across while expending as little energy as possible. I limited my speaking to only the things that had caused me a considerable amount of suffering that day. My mum could not answer me and I was unable to open my eyes while I uttered the words. I just said them and hoped that she would understand. Any other communication was performed through hand signals if possible, but I used very few of these as the energy it took to simply point would immediately drain me to the point of agony.

I could hardly move without a wave of exhaustion flooding over me. Once I finally started my treatment at the day clinic, taking the trip into and out of the place every day felt as though I was in the middle of a war, marching into battle. Although this seems like a severe explanation, these words are no overstatement. The procedure was carried out very precisely, step by step, to make the transition as smooth as possible. My mum and I had it down to a fine art.

She would drag me from my bed into the wheelchair and push me down to the car as fast as possible in silence. Timing was everything as, by this point, even slouching down was a struggle for me. She would then pull me up and into the car as I had no energy to complete the task myself. I had the seat laying back so that I didn't have to sit upright. It would take a minute or two to get into the clinic's parking lot. The same process was then repeated at top speed and I was wheeled into a secluded, darkened room and put back into bed. All of this was accomplished with an eye mask in place in order to shield me from light and movement whilst also wearing industrial strength ear defenders to protect me from noise.

I was now having to wear both of these apparatuses during every moment of the day as I could no longer stand any sort of sight or sound at all. The latter sensation was harder to deal with, as it always had been. If I heard even the tiniest of noises the intensity of my symptoms would push me over the edge. I could also take absolutely no touch. Occasionally, when I ached so badly from a lack of any connection that I was unable to stand it any longer, I would hold out my hand and stretch my index finger out to my mum. She would do the same and touch the tips of our fingers together for a couple of seconds until I could bear it no more. This later became known to us as 'ET fingers'.

My physician's long-term treatment plan for Lyme disease was to administer antibiotics intravenously six days a week. For all of the viral co-infections I would be given the same antiviral pill that the doctors in California and Michigan were prescribing. Before giving me either of the medications, she decided that it would be in my best interest to focus on building up my nutrients. While I had been waiting for admission into the day clinic, I had been tested for deficiencies. The results were startling. My doctor had been working with cases such as mine for decades and yet told my mother that she had rarely seen a person severely lacking in so many nutrients.

Over the last month my mum had been asked to keep a food journal for me. Although admittedly limited by this stage, my diet was still varied enough for it to not take the blame for the entirety of this issue. After reading through the results of all of my tests, it was concluded that the problem was malabsorption; my body was not absorbing the nutrients from the food I ate well enough. The tests also showed that I had a very bad case of candida along with an extremely low level of secretory IgA in my stomach; two issues that had been discovered while working with the nutritionist in the previous London centre. Having continuously low levels of sIgA can be a sign of an ongoing infection such as an unresolved virus.

The doctor explained that providing me with the vitamins and minerals that I was lacking beforehand would supply my body with the required strength to assimilate the drugs more readily once I began taking them. At the present time this high level of deficiency meant that my body was too weak. Going about it in this order would give the medicine a much more favourable chance of working and also lessen its side effects. We had to do it properly, step by step. On my first day at the clinic, the nurses inserted an IV into a vein in my arm within the first few minutes. Upon opening my eyes for a split second, I could see the bag of nutrients that was hanging above. I felt pure jubilation that a substance was being infused into my body that was going to help me to feel better. I burst into tears and cried softly for as long as my body could physically cope with the expression. It was such a huge comfort and so reassuring to finally have some sort of support.

For the next few months, I spent my days hooked up to IVs of various supplements, praying for the time when I would begin to feel any sort of improvement. I was fighting as hard as my mind and body could fight and giving every ounce of myself in order to make it through each moment. You've heard of the saying 'Time flies when you're having fun'. Well, the opposite is true when you are living in hell. Every minute felt like an eternity. I made it through the relentless agony by using all the strength that I could muster and acknowledging that the torment I was in was only temporary. For the first time in six years, I was now receiving proper treatment for my illness from a doctor who I had full faith in. I had made it this far, there was no way I was going to stop now, at what I believed was the last leg of the race.

CHAPTER 6
THIS ISN'T A SUMMER CAMP

I waited for the nutrients to build slowly within me, trusting that one day soon my body would begin to strengthen. Taking everything into consideration, I was as patient as I possibly could be with the process. Just having my IV hooked up and changed when I couldn't even take gentle touch was unspeakably difficult to bear. And although the nurses were careful to keep it to a minimum, the small amount of sound that I was able to hear from them following their daily routines was deafening. Even with my large industrial strength ear defenders on I was in a perpetual state of agony.

After eight weeks of having a needle inserted into my veins every day they finally began to collapse. For another month I had to endure the IV needle taking anywhere from 5 to 10 minutes to put in each time, something that would have been awful for even a healthy person to deal with. Eventually, my doctor recommended that I have a port surgically placed into my arm. This meant that an IV would no longer need to be inserted in the usual way. Once I became aware that such a device existed, my first thoughts were, 'Why did she delay this decision for so long?' All that I could assume was that she had been waiting for my body to get stronger before I had the operation. Since the expected improvement still hadn't happened, I was sent to the hospital to have the surgery.

It was a fairly quick procedure and I was given anaesthesia so wasn't aware of much of it at all. Having said that, the hospital was a half an hour trip away from my home and during my stay I had to face an abundance of sensory stimuli from noise to sight to touch. When I came around from the anaesthesia, my energy had been seriously depleted . Alongside that, I felt extremely nauseous and agonisingly ill. The entire day was horrific, from start to finish, but I put up with every single aspect of it. This was because I viewed it as another step towards becoming well, and I would have done *anything* to make that wish come true. I was willing to give 110% of myself; precisely what I was now doing.

Although I will never forget how hard that experience was, the resulting benefit was worth the pain. Instead of using a vein, the IV needle now only needed to be poked through a thin layer of skin in my arm before it reached the port. There is an art to finding the right spot but if carried out correctly, the process is very quick and almost painless. What used to be one of the worst parts of my day had become fairly simple. That is, as long as any of the nurses who could carry out the procedure easily attended to me. Unfortunately, there was one lady who would spend about the same amount of time to succeed as it had taken her before the operation. Each attempt she made was an overload on my senses as the sharpness of the needle repeatedly dug into my skin. Although she happened to be one of the sweetest and most gentle nurses in the clinic, I used to dread her coming into the room in the morning.

By now my body was reacting to foods so strongly that it was rejecting almost everything I ate. My meals mainly consisted of plain yoghurt, chicken, white rice and potatoes. On top of this diminutive list, I also managed a few different bland fruits and over-cooked vegetables. Every time I had diarrhoea, which had again become frequent, my stomach reacted more severely to everything I ingested for about a week afterwards. Because of this, I had to cut back on the already limited variety of foods and eat smaller meals for that length of time. Otherwise I would continue to have diarrhoea, making my body even weaker than it already was.

To help with the issue, my doctor prescribed low-dose immunotherapy, a treatment that supports people with Crohn's disease, food allergies and food sensitivities. It even works to combat many types of environmental allergies. My mum personally spoke with numerous patients at the day clinic that, after receiving the innovative vaccines, had been able to resume eating a nutritious and balanced diet. These were people who had literally been on death's door, all because of their bodies' adverse reaction to food. The premise of low-dose immunotherapy is that if the body is given a specific allergen in a tiny dose, it can learn how to neutralise it over time. Therefore, when it is later introduced properly, such as by eating a previously offending food for instance, the element is able to be dealt with appropriately, all former symptoms having been eliminated.

The nurses spent every morning testing me for individual allergens. They did this by injecting a tiny amount of each of the many specific foods into my body repeatedly in decreasing doses. If I had any type of reaction it was documented down. The most common response was a lasting redness at the injection site but there were many other symptoms including nausea, a lack of energy or general unwellness to a greater extent than I already had. A small measurement of the offending food was then added to a mixture of all of the others that had produced symptoms during the test phase. The concoction was given to my mum to inject into my leg once a day in the hopes that one day soon I would be able to eat again without consequence.

In order to reap the benefits of this therapy, I had to endure the testing procedure for a couple of hours each day for three whole months. During this period, a small needle was inserted into my thigh every ten minutes. Each time this was carried out the sharpness of the pain reverberated through my body, lowering my almost non-existent threshold to any sensation even further. I also had to deal with the varied and unpleasant symptoms that would often arise. I don't have enough words in my vocabulary to explain just how demanding it was for me to go through this process. Yet I put on my hard hat and went in, no matter how gruelling it was.

When I look back now it makes me feel physically sick to think about the level of exertion it took and the strain it all had on me. I really don't know how I kept going. The same thoughts were running through my head at the time; 'How can I carry on withstanding this?' People have since said to me, 'You are such a strong person to have gone through what you did'. In reality, I don't think I did have the strength that it took to get through each of the days. I was actually slowly beginning to fall apart because of having to tolerate them. Regardless of this, I was aware that the only other alternative was to lay in my bed feeling unbearably ill for the rest of my life. That option did not exist for me.

I went through the pain of the injections and the energy crashes that they caused day after day, week after week, month after month because I thought that eventually I would be able to eat nutritious meals again. By this point I was severely hungry and weak all of the time. I didn't know what to do with myself. I desperately needed to be able to find a moment's peace from it all but unfortunately there was nowhere for me to run. Because my body was lacking so many nutrients, my head was constantly in pain and existed in a thick fog which made it impossible for me to focus at all. I couldn't hold on to a train of thought as the energy it took to carry out this simple action wasn't there. I was certain that I would rather go through the extra anguish that the injections were causing me if it was going to result in me not having to feel all of this pain.

By the time I commenced treatment at the day clinic, my breathing difficulties had noticeably intensified. Each breath I took was leaving me feeling as though I was starving for oxygen, like I was permanently breathing into a paper bag. In order to address this, I was first given a variety of intricate tests geared towards my specific symptoms. After reviewing my results, the specialist discovered that I had something called respiratory alkalosis, a condition that is commonly found in those who are critically ill. All I had ever been told by GPs was that my breathlessness was due to low grade panic attacks (even though I had no other associated symptoms and my air hunger was experienced continuously throughout the day). Up until this point, I had never had any tests performed on my lungs or heart. These new doctors had provided me with yet another wonderful gift of knowledge. Because of their recognition of the validity of my illness and their impressive expertise, I was again able to see clearly, in black and white, what was malfunctioning within my body. After being breathless to the point of not being able to say a sentence without having to stop to take in more air, it felt highly gratifying to at last have test results confirming what I had already known all along; that there was a real physical reason for this terrible symptom. The tests had revealed that my oxygen levels were high while, on the other hand, my carbon dioxide was dangerously low. We were alerted to just how serious a situation it had become. My body was too weak to be able to breathe deeply enough to create enough CO_2. By now my level of exhaustion was so elevated that even the movement it took to inhale and exhale was extremely taxing on me. As a result, I was breathing very shallowly.

My doctor responded immediately and gave me something called a CPAP mask. The apparatus was meant to retrain my body to take in less oxygen and generate more CO_2 with each breath. I was instructed to wear it for six hours interspersed throughout the day, seven days a week. From the moment I first put it on, I considered it to be a torture device and honestly, I still do.

The item was similar to a full face snorkel mask as the wearer's mouth area was included within the enclosure as well as their nose. It was meant to be suctioned to the head and strapped around it as tight as it could go so that there were no gaps for air to escape. There was a long, narrow tube coming out from an area at the bottom; the only place where oxygen was able to enter and leave. The tube was about the length of a person's arm with the circumference and opening at the end being no bigger than a ten pence coin. The air required to breathe had to make it through that tiny space and travel the long distance up to the mask. In order for it to reach their nose, the wearer would have to breathe in as hard as they possibly could. Only then were they able to receive the tiny amount of oxygen that they would need to stay alive.

Because of my utter inability to communicate with others, it wasn't possible for anyone to explain to me what I could expect or how the device was going to feel beforehand. All I knew from the minimal words that my mum had used the day before was that my carbon dioxide levels were low and there was a solution for this problem: 'CO2 low, treatment tomorrow'. Upon hearing these four words, I had felt reassured that finally some help was going to be provided.

I visualised the treatment to be some form of air that when I breathed in, would provide me with immediate relief and satisfy my incessant yearning. Instead, the mask was strapped tightly around my head and I instantly felt as though I couldn't breathe at all. Naturally, I panicked and cried out 'Can't breathe' through the piece of plastic that was suctioned onto me. All I could think was that there had to be something faulty with the mask. Or maybe they had forgotten to turn on the machine that produced the much-needed air that I had imagined I would receive. I needed to get that monstrous thing off of my face quickly before I passed out from a lack of oxygen.

As it turns out, this harsh contrast from my optimistic assumption was completely normal and to be expected. With the specialist using as little words as possible, I was told that this was what I would have to put up with every single day for the foreseeable future; 'It's OK. Leave it on.' The panic I felt, believing that if someone didn't remove the mask quickly I would surely suffocate to death, turned into utter disbelief. I was meant to feel like this for *six hours*? How was that humanly possible?

From the first moment it was put on, I had no idea how I was going to leave that mask on my face for another minute. But like the good girl that I was, I followed their instructions. To this day, when I think about that contraption it sends shivers down my spine. It felt like I had my head in a plastic bag with a seal around my neck. Every breath was a struggle, like I was slowly suffocating over the six hours. Yet I had to make the decision to willingly strap it on my head, day after day, for months to come. Again, what kept me dedicated to the task was the notion that it was my only option if I wanted to be well. By this time, my postural hypertension had become so severe that I was constantly having to lay flat. I couldn't even sit reclined for more than a few seconds without collapsing. My doctor theorised that my body had become so accustomed to being immobilised that it no longer had the capacity to respond when I made any improvement. She attributed this to be why there had been no change in my health after all of the months I had spent receiving her various forms of treatment. Her reasoning meant that I might now have the ability to sit up but my body had simply forgotten how to manage this simple feat.

To combat this suspected automatic reaction, she had me begin to lay at a small incline by raising my bed at the top half by approximately a couple of inches at a time. My body did adjust to each small modification in the end. Although, in order for this to happen I had to endure an agony worse than death, or so I imagined it to be. I find it very difficult to distinguish each of my individual physical states. This particular one manifested itself as how I picture it would feel to be drained of almost all of your blood. I felt immense wooziness and weakness, the feeling in my head was unbearably painful, I could not think or concentrate, and my exhaustion and viral malaise had been multiplied by ten. The reaction would last for no less than a week each time my bed was raised ever so slightly. This series of events was repeated about five times before my body stopped being able to adjust to the changes. All of the stress and strain that I withstood for weeks on end only ever resulted in me being able to lay at a very slight incline.

In an additional attempt to awaken my body to the presumed changes that had already taken place, my physician also asked me to stand for approximately 15 seconds a few times per day. Every time

I endeavoured to do this, I was on the edge of collapsing from the very first moment I got up. The sensation would build over the handful of seconds that I could manage to sustain my upright posture before I slumped back into bed. It would then take me about an hour to recover. My mum made sure to always stand directly by my side in case I fell over. None of this effort ever helped me, even slightly.

In carrying out all of these methods simultaneously over the months, I was continuously facing so many different forms of hell. I was overexerting myself way past my limits, both physically and psychologically. Even so, I kept pushing and fighting as hard as I could to make it through to the end of each day. I recognise that it may have simply been my extremely weak state that was causing each of the techniques to be as horrendous as they were. No matter the reason, I was living every moment at breaking point.

I longed for the clinic to say that they were going to start the *real* treatment. Every time that I entered the building I prayed to hear the word 'antibiotics'. Four months into receiving the nutrient infusions, there was still no breakthrough in my health. After waiting this long in vain, my physician eventually decided that the time had come, no matter what state I was in. It had become obvious to her that I was not going to improve with alternative therapies alone.

The night before she disclosed her new plan, I had a dream. In it, a doctor examined me and then proceeded to say, 'You will take several medications on your healing journey before you become well. The first medicine will begin tomorrow.' The next morning, I went into the clinic completely unaware of what was to happen. After hoping with all of my heart, month after month, the long-awaited words were uttered at long last. Was the materialisation of my dream simply a fortuitous coincidence? I will never know.

I then began to receive intravenous antibiotics six days a week. I said a silent prayer every time the bag was hooked up to my port. I was finally being given a form of treatment that had been proven by research studies to be a cure for my disease. This recent headway restored my confidence and with it my patience.

I had been prescribed medication for the Lyme, but I also needed something to address the many co-infections that I had, including the Epstein-Barr virus. About a month afterwards, my physician decided that it was the right time for me to begin taking antiviral pills. I was delighted that I was going to be given another form of 'real' medicine in order to treat a large part of what was causing me to feel so ill. Surely this would increase my chances of feeling better in the near future. I welcomed any level of relief from my symptoms with open arms.

However, because of my severe stomach issues, I could not keep the antiviral tablets inside of me, no matter how hard I persisted. Every time I took the new pill, it would cause a terrible stomach ache followed by diarrhoea. After only a couple of days I had to stop trying. I was so incredibly disappointed. My doctor reassured my mother by telling her that soon the immunotherapy would begin to work, and my stomach would stop reacting to foreign substances. I would then be able to resume the antiviral medication. She even went so far as to create a new vaccine of the specific drug just for me. I began my special injection and waited as patiently as I could for circumstances to change.

When the promised six-month timespan was up, my father was unable to continue to live in the house we had left behind. It was obvious to all of us that my recovery was going to take much longer than we had originally supposed. This turn of events had no effect on me since I would continue to lie in a bed in silence no matter where we lived, but for my mum it was an enormous disappointment. She was miles away from home, caring for me 24 hours a day with no source of support nearby and no end in sight. It was then that she had to make the difficult decision to rehome all of our pets as there was no other option.

When considering the trials of someone living with a long-term illness, those who haven't experienced it for themselves may not realise the amount of uncomfortable circumstances that must be faced. There are so many painful decisions that have to be made solely out of necessity rather than choice. For us, giving up our pets was one such situation. Luckily, we found friends and family members to take them in. My dogs had been like my children, they meant more to me than almost anything. Because of my level of deterioration, I had minimal knowledge about all that was taking place, and honestly, I had no energy left in me to care. The fact that there is any truth to that last sentence illustrates just how all-consuming my illness had become.

Despite having received so many varied forms of treatment, after attending the clinic six days a week for over nine months, there had been no progression in my health whatsoever. Even the revered antibiotics had been unsuccessful in creating a shift in me within the five months that I had now been taking them. When I used the CPAP mask, I actually noticed a decline in the quality of my breathing over the many months. I had my mum relate that fact when she went to each of my weekly progress appointments. But no matter what she said, my physician was adamant that things would turn around. We were informed that this magnification of my symptoms was commonplace at first. Therefore, I needed to remain persistent with the mask. I put my trust in her and followed the given advice.

I wore that torture device for hours at a time, every day for eight tedious months. It took me that long before I finally decided to experiment by taking a temporary break. Within the first few days I already saw a marked improvement in my breathlessness that quickly reverted back to where it had been before I started the treatment. This, on top of the fact that I was no longer expending the required energy to willingly suffocate for six hours of the day, meant that life became markedly easier for me. I decided that I would not wear it again. Oddly, my doctor still did not agree that the mask had been in any way disadvantageous. Instead, she expressed her obvious annoyance at my non-compliance.

The immunotherapy vaccines also ended up causing an adverse

response not long afterwards. During the months that I had been using them my stomach had never strengthened, not even a little bit. I had tried new foods here and there at the insistence of my physician but my body continued to react to them in the manner in which it always had. But the real problem had begun during the last allergy test that the nurses carried out. Within minutes I experienced a severe reaction at the injection site and a crash in my energy levels. After that, my stomach became so sensitive that even the vaccine that had been tailored specifically for me began to give me diarrhoea. As my mother continued, on doctor's orders, to inject me each day, my stomach grew ever more fragile. No matter what she said to the medical team, they replied with the same answer; keep going. The situation became ever more dire until, at the worst point, I ended up spending seven days without being able to eat any food at all. That week I was truly afraid. On day five, I mustered up all the energy that I could to ask my mum, 'Am I going to die?' All she could say in reply was, 'I don't know.' Previously, I may not have been able to pinpoint what was going to happen to me or where I would end up, but I had never, for one moment, thought that there was any risk of death. For the first time, that question had become relevant.

During this fearful period, my doctor maintained that I *must* keep having the injections. She was emphatic that the revered immunotherapy was not to blame for why my stomach had become so dangerously weak. Regardless of how many times my mum tried to tell her that it was obviously so, she was unwavering on this point and made clear to us that under no circumstances was I to stop using them. I must continue on as they were the only solution for me to be able to eat again.

I knew that what she was saying was wrong and yet at the same time felt too afraid to ignore her instructions and follow my own heart. After what I had experienced with the CPAP mask, it may seem silly to have made the same mistake so quickly after the last, but you see, I had put all of my trust into this doctor and believed that surely she would know what she was talking about better than I.

My reasoning was based on the fact that she had seen countless patients with similar conditions to my own. I felt petrified that if I stopped listening to her instructions, I would end up dead. I continued with the injections, my symptoms increasing in severity every day, until I reached a point in which I realised that if I kept going in this fashion, I *would* soon be buried six feet underground. After a week spent without any food, hardly any water and the fear of having to be admitted into hospital looming over me, I made the difficult decision to go against my doctor's wishes for the second time and discontinue the treatment.

Very soon after this action was taken, it became possible for me to eat tiny bites of puréed boiled chicken and white rice. Although this was good news, I could only manage one teaspoonful every ten minutes for about an hour at a time before needing a long break to rest my acutely sensitive stomach. This didn't add up to very much food by the end of the day. I had become so weak that I could no longer feed myself. I felt like a baby bird as my mum spoon fed me the mushed-up food that she had prepared. The blending was done not only to help my stomach in the digestion process but also so I didn't have to chew as by this time even that small act was too much for me to bear.

Over time, I was slowly able to increase my food intake and with that my self-care but by this point my stomach had been weakened beyond repair. I tried the vaccine once more, a few weeks later but its harmful effects became immediately evident. It was such a sad realisation that almost everything that had been provided by the clinic to help me had ended up harming me even further.

I haven't the words to describe the level of torment that I was feeling. I was now left to deal with the agonising aftermath of my body's extreme deterioration on top of the feelings of terror I had over what was to become of me. I lived every day in a state of turmoil. One day, after talking with my mum, another physician suggested that it might be a good idea for me to take a break from the numerous forms of treatment or, he envisaged, my overloaded body might begin to reject all of the assistance that it was being given. That was when my mum informed him that this was already happening.

Every single day during the nine months that I had been a patient at the clinic, I had endured such high levels of bodily exertion and psychological anguish, on top of a relentlessly gruelling schedule, that the burden had finally become too great. I felt that I had gone way past the limit of what I could give of myself in terms of effort. In the months leading up to this moment I would constantly wonder, 'How much longer can I possibly withstand this?' As each day ended, I didn't think I could make it through the next, but I kept going because I couldn't see any other choice.

It had now gotten to the point where I knew explicitly that if something didn't change soon, I would suffer a mental breakdown. Or maybe I already had. I had passed the point where I could no longer cope, having pushed myself for so many months when instead I should have stopped. And all because of wanting more than anything to be well. The trouble was that my mind could not survive under these circumstances. I was living this existence all alone, consumed by my own thoughts day after day, with no form of sight, sound or touch; absolutely no stimuli to provide me with the awareness that I was even a part of the outside world. It had become very hard to tell exactly how I was feeling when all that existed for me now was the darkness inside my own head. This blackness was all consuming and in its voraciousness had devoured everything I knew, everything I was.

It was clear to me that I needed a rest. Even when I stayed home the one day a week that the clinic was closed, my coping abilities would increase. When my mother shared my point of view with my doctor her reply was, 'This isn't a summer camp. If she wants to get well, she cannot decide to stop and start whenever it suits her.' She disagreed with me needing any respite and expressed her strong opinion that if I took the time off, I would never get well.

Her conviction was stated with full awareness that there was the possibility for me to continue to have the antibiotics intramuscularly.

This particular form of the medicine only needed to be injected into my body twice weekly, meaning that I could make the short trip to and from the clinic on those occasions and remain at home for the rest of the time. I was more than happy to make use of this option.

My doctor was being completely unsupportive of my urgent request. She had been the first healthcare provider to take my situation into careful consideration and the first to believe in the real presence of my physiological illness. Yet for some reason, since attending her clinic, all of my input had been brushed aside. From the beginning I had held such high hopes that she would be different. But in the end, it boiled down to the same problem; no medical professional would listen to me, no matter how hard I tried to make myself heard.

My practitioner proceeded to inform my mum that she was thinking of having me sectioned, explaining that any doctor in the NHS would have done this a long time ago. She respected my illness but at the same time wondered if the reason why I was not responding to her treatments was because there was a part of me that didn't want it to happen. By now I had become all too familiar with this automatic response from doctors. They seem to have no problem placing the blame onto their patient as soon as they are unable to find an answer themselves. But I had never expected this from her.

Upon hearing my physician's stance, my mother felt both disbelief and shock. How could the woman who had personally tested and diagnosed me herself be saying those words? My mum made the decision to keep this volatile information from me, realising that if I was made aware of the threat of being admitted into a mental health facility, I might actually need to be in one.

How anyone could make such a radical assumption without ever having spoken to me, I will never understand. There was no way for me to demonstrate my unambiguous grasp of reality. Without being able to speak, I was unable to explain that every one of my physical symptoms was real, none of it was being created in my mind and that all I had ever wanted, more than anything in the world, was to be well. If I could have, I would have told my doctor that I had been working towards that single goal for the last seven years, fighting my hardest, doing everything I possibly could, to the point of mental collapse in order to achieve it. That was exactly the reason why I was where I found myself now; completely drained, emotionally wrecked and desperately needing a breather.

I felt trapped, as though I was laying on the ground with a ton of bricks upon my chest. I was fighting as hard as I could to get up while people stood over me shouting 'Do more. Work harder. What you are doing is not enough'. I struggled hour after hour, day after day, with no end in sight but there was no way I could pull myself out from underneath the rubble. My existence was confined within a state of inescapable silence. I wished that I could scream from the top of my lungs that I *was* trying with *every* fibre of my being. Instead, I was being forced to swallow others' distorted views and condemning words while having no way of expressing my truth. This feeling of oppression went on to haunt me long after my struggle was over.

Under doctor's orders, after a couple of weeks spent at home, a psychiatrist made a home visit in order to assess whether I should be admitted into a psychiatric hospital. It was my understanding that a person was coming to observe that I was still of sound mind. As a result of this, I would then be allowed to stay home temporarily. This explanation enabled me to comprehend the importance of the meeting without putting me into a state of deep fear and panic.

Luckily, because of my previous weeks of rest, I had now built up enough strength to manage to project a handful of words per day. During the doctor's visit, I used up any and all of my resources to verbalise a few sentences and listen to him gently and slowly say a few back. This was carried out over a ten-minute period with many breaks interspersed in between in order for me to try and gather up some more energy.

The psychiatrist was such a kind and understanding man who genuinely cared about my welfare. Once he had carried out his short assessment, he left the room only to cry with my mum over how desperately sad my existence had become. He was able to conclude very quickly that I was of sound mind and that there was no reason for any concern.

Thank goodness for me, he had actually listened to everything that I had to say and taken my feelings into account. He told my mother that he completely agreed with my sentiments and thought that any person in my situation would need a serious rest after all that I had sustained. After his visit, he went back to my practitioner and explained this rationale to her. Because of his attentiveness and ability to sympathise with how I felt, I was afforded a well-earned rest.

I then began to travel into the clinic twice a week so that I could receive the new form of antibiotic treatment. I felt pleased with this, despite the medicine having to be administered by inserting two giant needles into my buttocks. The fact that I felt any happiness about this was a clear testament to how grateful I was to be given some time to regroup. I didn't see what I was doing as giving up. My plan was to resume my full-time schedule at the day clinic as soon as possible. I presumed that this would happen in about six weeks.

The purpose of taking the respite was so that I could recapture my inner strength, an aspect that was essential to my healing. I now had some time to recharge my battery and my soul in order to continue the fight, not that the war ever truly stopped for me. Just getting through the agony of each moment, regardless of where my body lay, was a battle in itself.

In the end, the arrangement was to last for four whole months as an unexpected obstacle was placed in my path. Only a few weeks into my rest period, my stomach worsened dramatically and I began to find it difficult to eat again. These incessant symptoms progressed until, in the end, I was having trouble digesting any food at all. The substantial reduction of my intake of nutrients meant that I could no longer handle the short trip to and from the clinic every few days. It also became impossible for me to withstand the daily commotion that went on inside the building. Stopping all treatment became an unavoidable consequence of my body's further degeneration.

At this point, my doctor discharged me from her care, explaining to my mum that she could no longer keep an eye on me from home. It felt very frightening to be left all alone at my most vulnerable point. I could only hope that in time my body would begin to recover so that I could then be reinstated as a patient once again.

I am disappointed to have to write that nothing prescribed in the day clinic ever had a positive effect on my health. I was a patient there for thirteen months in total. Within that time, I used the CPAP mask for eight months, had supplements given to me intravenously for nine, four months of food allergy injections, nine months of antibiotics for Lyme disease and had attempted to take the antiviral drug for my many co-infections without any luck.

I will never be able to say why all of these innovative treatments did not help me. The plethora of inspiring stories that my mother was told by other patients were what had kept us going through some of the darkest moments. I suspect that my body was simply not strong enough to handle all of the vigorous treatments that were administered in such a short space of time. This was definitely how it had felt whilst I had been in the throes of it all.

I have since been told by another doctor that my opinion makes total sense from a medical standpoint. Before an operation, the surgeons want their patients to be in the best physical shape possible in order for the surgery to have the greatest chance of success. The procedure will be demanding on the body and so the more robust the individual is from the outset, the better likelihood they will have for it to run smoothly and to recover without complication. This concept remains the same for any form of medical care. As I had commenced all of my treatments in such an acutely weak state, none of them had been given much of a chance of producing positive results.

The futile struggle that I personally underwent is a perfect illustration of the crucial importance of early detection and treatment of Lyme disease. If more doctors were to heed their patients' cries for help and follow on with a thorough investigation into the infection, countless numbers of people would have the chance to be rehabilitated. The blatant disregard that is so common today is continuing to allow the illness to become chronic. If any one of the first handful of doctors I had seen had possessed the wherewithal to seriously consider Lyme disease, I would not have found myself anywhere near to the mess that I was in now.

CHAPTER 7
USE YOUR WORDS

I had been thrown back into deep waters. Only this time I was all alone in my bed, without any form of medical support. The only food I could manage to eat now was a small amount of white rice that was blended into a paste consistency, so as to give my body a chance to digest it. I became that baby bird once more, my mother standing over me with her spoonfuls of mush.

I could handle a very tiny mouthful of food approximately once every ten minutes. If I listened to my desperate urges and attempted to have any more than that, my stomach would emit squealing noises soon afterwards. Alongside the pain that followed, they were a clear indication of imminent diarrhoea. Each time that end result occurred, my stomach would become even more sensitive and the digestion process permanently more difficult, meaning that I would then have to eat less to avoid the cycle repeating itself. My main mission became to do anything I could to avoid having diarrhoea since I knew that if this pattern continued it would eventually lead to my death. It was a very scary place to be. I yearned to eat more than anything but as soon as I ingested too much food my body would immediately reject it.

I became hyper alert about how much of the goo I ate and how often. If there was the slightest sign of any discomfort, I would stop eating immediately and wait for the symptoms to subside. I thought that my stomach would begin to improve as long as I paid attention to it. That was what had happened the last time I had found myself in this frightening position. But this time no amount of attentiveness was causing it to heal. I, instead, became weaker and weaker as the weeks went by. I had no idea what to do. My only option seemed to be to continue on with the strategy and remain patient. To accomplish that particular state of being while living with the most intense suffering I had ever known felt impossible.

I hadn't anticipated the drawn-out starvation that I was now living through to be as intolerably painful as it was. Before experiencing it for myself, I had expected to feel a tremendous level of hunger but in reality, there was so much more to it. Yes, I was exceptionally hungry. I was desperate for food. I can remember lying in bed, conjuring up large beef burgers, doughnuts, cakes or any other food with a high fat, sugar or protein content. I would spend large portions of my day imagining them in detail. The process tortured me but my mind wouldn't focus on anything else.

As well as feeling a hunger beyond belief, my body was agonisingly painful, the most unbearable part being the aching in my head. I could hardly think, it felt as though my brain had shut down almost completely. I had become so utterly depleted and was dizzy, woozy and lethargic all of the time. The weakness I felt made me unable to cope with anything emotionally or physically at all.

After losing so much weight my body became skin and bones. I didn't even have the energy required to move anymore. My commode had always been right next to my bed but I no longer had the strength to use it on my own. My mum now had to come into the room so that she could lift me onto it and hold me up while I relieved myself. That simple task drained me of any and all of the energy that I had left and yet I was forced to face it repetitively throughout the day.

I decided adamantly that I did not want to go into hospital, even though my mother asked me every single day. I knew that at some point I was going to hear her frightened voice say, 'Hospital?' Just listening to that one word would send me into a whirlwind of pain as it zapped all of the energy from me. Each time she said it I would feel angry at her for the suffering it would cause mixed with a feeling of frustration from being unable to stop her. I understand now that her fear for my life was what had compelled her to say the word time after time. Completely alone in the room next to mine, my mum was having to watch as her daughter slowly starved to death. There was nothing she could do but wait.

Despite her pleas, my answer was always the same. I wanted to deal with the situation I now found myself in as best as I could on my own, being mindful that no doctor would be able to understand or respect my needs. I had heard horror stories about others being hospitalised with ME. My previous doctor had shared that if I was ever admitted into hospital the staff would completely disregard my symptoms and all of the tests that she had carried out. They would not listen to my mum when she attested to the fact that there was a physical reason for why I could not eat. Instead, they would undoubtedly have me sectioned, force feed me and do all sorts of other terrible things, believing that my condition was caused by an imbalance of the mind.

I wanted to live and be well. However, I had recently become aware that this fervent wish might not be possible for me anymore. And if given a choice to die in my bed rather than in a place that would take away every ounce of my autonomy, that was what I would do. Nothing would be worse than the level of powerlessness that would ensue if I became their patient. Not even death. I was now facing that very prospect and honestly, in comparison to what I was presently experiencing, it didn't feel like the worst thing that could happen to me. At least then the agony would end.

A couple of months into my starvation, my hair began to fall out from the severe lack of nutrition. I first noticed the heavy shedding when it began to build up on my pillow and the bed surrounding me. In the end it was coming out in clumps. In the past few years, my hair had grown all the way down my back. Sometimes I would imagine how when I was well I would be so happy about its length. To me this thought exemplifies what a positive mindset I still possessed. Even as I was wondering if I was going to die I was concurrently thinking, 'Won't I have lovely long hair when I get better'! Once it began to fall out in large chunks, I wished that I could scream, 'Does *everything* have to be wrenched away from me?'

Eventually, my stomach became so inflamed that I stopped being able to digest food altogether. After five days without any form of sustenance, following on from months of not much more than that, the pain that I was experiencing became so unbearable that I gave in. Even though I could still remember all of the horror stories about hospitalisation, the level of desperation in me became so great that I could no longer see straight. All of my logic and reasoning went out of the window as meeting my urgent needs for relief took control of my senses.

Logically, I knew that the easiest way out would be to let myself die. If I lived, all I would have to come back to was my cruel existence. But the level of pain that I felt was too strong. I was clutching on to anything that had the potential to release me from it. The next time my mum asked me her daily question, 'Hospital?' my answer was a feeble 'yes'.

My mum called a doctor's surgery without hesitation and a GP was sent out to the house. When he arrived, he spent five minutes looking me over. He then proceeded to tell her in a cold tone of voice that there was no need for me to go into hospital. Apparently, I could go on for weeks in this state without dying. He was eventually convinced to make the referral at my mum's insistence. It took three more days for the NHS hospital to send an ambulance out to the house. Within this time, my dad had travelled the few hours from his home to support both of us in any way that he could.

I thought some sort of help would surely be given to me shortly after my admittance. It didn't take long for me to realise that I had assumed wrongly. When I was finally offered a bed, I waited in it for three whole days before anything happened; three whole days spent in torment, praying for someone to come in and do *something*. When the staff eventually tested my glucose levels the results were dangerously low. This was what finally prompted them to take action; I was given a drip containing electrolytes. My sugars were checked routinely from then on.

A little while later, it was decided that I needed a feeding tube. My parents were told that the food was specially designed for problems of this nature and my stomach would be able to digest the slow but steady delivery of nutrition. I was thrilled. The fact that some nutrients would soon be entering my system was like a dream come true. I was eager to feel any form of relief from the excruciating pain. All of the physicians on my extensive team had emphatically decided that my symptoms, including my inability to eat, were due in entirety to a psychological impairment. They expressed their collective narrow-minded viewpoint to my parents regularly and made all of their medical decisions based upon this notion. The only reason that doctors entered my room was to periodically ask my mum to try and get me to eat some food, as if it was my choice to refrain. The fact that it had taken them days to offer any proper help whatsoever made their standpoint very clear.

The feeding tube was to be given to me on one condition. I was made to take my eye mask off, look a doctor in the eye and tell her that I would not eat a hospital meal and that I wanted the procedure done. These people had no idea what they were asking of me. I acquiesced to their demands, after listening to the lady explain with a voice that felt like razor blades that she would only agree because I was *refusing* to eat. I complied with her false statements and pleaded for the procedure, simply because there was no other choice.

I had been forced to speak to them in order to be able to receive the urgent and indispensable care that I needed, no matter that it went against all of my wishes and caused me severe physical distress. In their eyes, it was a simple request that I was completely capable of carrying out. They couldn't understand what all of the fuss was about.

Once I had abided by their authoritarian instruction, I was finally allowed to receive the help that I had been begging for. The invasive procedure was administered a whole five days after my admittance into hospital. I was completely aware during the entire process as I had been denied sedation. They put the feeding tube through one nostril and fed it down my oesophagus into my stomach. I have since wondered if my reaction to the process was worsened even more by the severely weakened state that I was in at the time. I guess I will never know but what I am sure of is that I was definitely not, in any way, prepared for what took place. I had pictured the event to be a little discomforting as the tube passed through my nose and throat but over so quickly that I would be able to handle it.

What actually took place was to be strikingly different. All of my nerves came alive as my body struggled to reject what was happening to it. For the several minutes that it took to thread the long, hollow piece of plastic through my oesophagus I felt as if I was being attacked by it. My body was doing its best to expel everything from all of the holes in my face at once. My eyes and my nose were streaming. I was retching. I was gagging. I was coughing. I was spitting and drooling everywhere. It felt like I was going to suffocate somehow, as if I had swallowed a large piece of food and was choking on it. My body and mind had gone into panic mode.

The procedure was an extremely traumatising experience, both physically and mentally. I could not understand why the doctors had been so inhumane by refusing to sedate my weakened body. In the state that I was in, it would have been so much easier for me to endure that way, but I suppose this wasn't a consideration of theirs. In their minds there was nothing wrong with me other than my 'refusal' to eat. Once it was over, I managed to glance up at the bag of liquid food that was being slowly passed through the cylindrical instrument into my stomach one drip at a time. It was such a solace for me to know that I was finally receiving some form of help.

Not more than two days passed before we were informed that I no longer needed the support as I had reached what they considered to be a 'safe weight'. The lengthy tube was then ripped out of me, as fast and as hard as an object could be taken out of a person's body. Picture one sweeping motion. From this, my body suffered a repeat episode of shock and, on top of that, a painful friction burn which has permanently scarred my throat and, to this day, still causes me discomfort.

The nurse that carried out the second procedure had made it absolutely clear from the get go that she had no sympathy for me or my situation. She conveyed this to us on a regular basis when in conversation with my parents and through the careless manner in which she interacted with me while on duty, going out of her way to treat me as if I was an average patient with no sensory sensitivities whatsoever.

I felt greatly dismayed by my medical team's decision to remove my only source of nutrients at a time when my inability to digest food had not wavered even slightly. I couldn't fathom the point of having to go through that disturbing experience when the benefits of it had been taken away from me no more than two days afterwards. At a later date, while looking through my medical records, I discovered that whilst in their care I had been given a diagnosis of anorexia nervosa. Reading those two words vindicated what I had easily deduced from their callous behaviour; they had made up their minds that it was my choice not to eat regardless of the fact that I had, at the very same moment, been *begging* them for help.

My positive Lyme disease and co-infection test results had been completely disregarded by the team. The doctors refused to pay attention to them, simply because the specific testing methods were not used within the NHS. My parents went on to try and prove that I did, in fact, have the disease by providing a list of my numerous symptoms. Their predictably imperceptive response was that it was impossible to have the number and extremity of symptoms that I had on such a global scale. In the minds of these medical professionals, the named infection only attacked one part of the body at a time. If only they could have been aware of the countless number of people who had suffered just as I was suffering, with these same 'global' symptoms, that had eventually been successfully treated for Lyme disease in progressive clinics around the world.

The doctors' next decree was for me to see a psychiatrist. This course of action had been determined even though it had been explained very clearly that I could not speak or be spoken to without it causing me remarkable pain and energy loss. My mum relayed to me, as best as she could, that if I didn't speak with the mental health professional I would be at risk of being committed. I was deeply afraid as I had no idea how I was going to accomplish the inordinate task.

When the time came, I managed to say one short sentence and the psychiatrist spoke back to me for about half a minute. It felt like torture to have to make it through those 30 seconds. During that period, she explained that she would come in each day for increasingly longer stretches of time. She insisted that, through talk therapy alone, I would become well. Wow, it was that simple. Why hadn't I thought of that seven years ago? (Insert sarcasm here).

The next step was to give me a mental health assessment. My parents were told that if I was unable to pass it, I would be put into a psychiatric unit. God only knows what they would do to me there. I was fully aware that if I was given the assessment it would end in failure. Without the ability to communicate there was no way for me to demonstrate to them how highly cognisant I was. I lay waiting in the hospital bed, spending all of my thinking moments wondering whether I was going to be locked away.

My parents were spoken to with complete disrespect and rudeness the entire time we were there. They were even blamed for my circumstances. The doctors insisted that I was only ill because they had been believing my story and giving in to my requests. My mother was informed that our time together would be limited by the hospital staff. They would only allow her to see me during short scheduled intervals. Once they separated us, they assumed that I would begin to heal from the mental illness that they were certain I had.

My mum was the person who had been right by my side every step of the way. I can't imagine how she must have felt as a parent and a caregiver, to have had to listen to herself be held accountable, yet again, for all of the suffering that I had endured. All the while, I lay starving in the hospital bed next door.

Upon hearing the latest news, I felt my high anxiety turn into pure panic. My mum was my only buffer from the bombardment to my senses that was taking place in that hospital on a regular basis. She was also the only person that knew how I felt and the only one who could make sense of my extremely condensed paraphrasing or read my sign language whenever I had to express an urgent need. Most importantly, she was my only protection from the domineering doctors and nurses who were determined to force their skewed initiatives upon me. She was my shield from it all. Without her, I would be utterly defenceless.

The doctors started using intimidation tactics. They informed my parents that if the medical team classed me as a vulnerable adult, we would no longer have any say in matters. The hospital would then be able to do anything they liked. Upon hearing this, my father told them that if that happened, he would remove me from the hospital. Their immediate response was to relay a similar case that had been in the newspapers not long before which had resulted in the parent being put into jail.

I was having to play a game. We all were. There was much talk about having me sectioned. My mum warned me repeatedly to follow whatever the doctors said as there was no way for me to explain that I was 100% rational. I knew that I had to speak to the psychiatrist as it was the only way I was going to prove that I was of sound mind. Yet I equally understood that there was no way that it was going to be possible. I wished for the capacity to be able to scream in their faces that I had a real, quantifiable physical illness that was causing every one of my symptoms. The fact that I couldn't get that across to anybody was exasperating.

I was trapped, completely defenceless, with no way out of this mess.

That realisation frightened me tremendously. My decision to be admitted into hospital had been a monumental mistake. The only action the staff had taken so far was to insert a feeding tube inside of me for a couple of days. Of course, I would rather not have been subjected to that traumatic experience for the 48 hours of tube formula that I had received in return.

Because of the pervasive disbelief that existed over my physical illness, the hospital staff would not take into regard the adverse reaction that occurred whenever I was exposed to sight, sound, or touch. The bright hospital lights were left on in my room. Nurses bustled in and out, talking to me as if I was no different to any of the other patients they saw in the day, shouting to make themselves heard beyond my ear defenders. They touched me very roughly whenever they needed to carry out any tests, not realising that all of their insensitivity was, by this stage, literally killing me.

Some of them demonstrated an added twist of malice that I can only assume came from the sentiment that I was a waste of their time and resources. The doctor who was in charge of the ward that I was on unsympathetically commanded that I take off my headphones which, other than my earplugs, were the only instruments safeguarding me from noise. She also proclaimed that if I didn't take off the eye mask that was protecting me from the invasive light and movement, it would signify to them that I was 'making a conscious choice to retreat from the world'. She spoke with absolutely no appreciation for the consequences that I would face upon removing both of these indispensable aids.

When I took them both off, my head felt a higher level of pressure and my energy became lower than I had ever experienced before. When my parents shared what was happening with the psychiatrist, she informed them that, although the doctor was acting as if her commands were compulsory, she had absolutely no authority to demand anything of the sort from me. My ear defenders and eye mask were placed back on my head without a moment's delay.

That same tyrant of a doctor's next endeavour was to force me to speak. By now, my mum had learned how to deftly infer my limited use of language and hand signals and could therefore execute each of my specific requests with ease. The hospital did not like this at all. They saw it, along with any speaking that my mum carried out on my behalf, as highly unhealthy behaviour that only escalated our 'co-dependent' relationship. The consensus amongst the team was that my mental disturbance would improve once I began to communicate my needs on my own.

The nurses were instructed to disregard my very simple requests unless I 'spoke properly'. Their response to my desperate pleas became, 'You need to use your words, we can't understand you unless you do, use complete sentences now' in a condescending tone as if they were talking to a two-year-old. For me to try and push out a sentence felt worse than death. This unnecessary sensation could then last for hours afterwards. Nevertheless, I was made to comply with these demands even when I had already made what I required obvious. For example, if I had to use the toilet I said 'toilet', or if I needed an extra blanket I said 'cold', but the painful exercise would ensue anyway.

I was confounded by the staff's brazen obstinacy and petrified of what was to come. I wanted to leave the hospital desperately and get back to the safe confines of my own bedroom. If it meant that I had to die in my bed, I didn't care. I could no longer bear the intolerable disrespect that was being dished out on a regular basis, nor the torturous consequences that followed. On top of that, the very real danger of being put into a psychiatric facility loomed over me. However, I couldn't be discharged from the hospital without a doctor agreeing to sign the paperwork to release me. I pleaded to be allowed to go home but they refused. I had been cornered into their captivity. The powerlessness that I felt in that hospital was something that continued to torment me for years after I left its four walls.

After carrying out some blood tests, the doctors told my parents the results verified that nothing was medically wrong with my stomach.

This was all that was needed for them to conclude that I was refraining from eating by choice. Because of their findings, they would not refer me to the gastroenterology ward or provide me with any further form of support. Instead, they continued to pressure me to eat.

What they didn't understand was that every single time I had diarrhoea there would be less of a chance that I would ever be able to eat again. In effect, the doctors were unwittingly encouraging me to kill myself. For the first time, I would not follow their orders, knowing full well that if I did so I would no longer be alive. I refused to eat more than my stomach allowed me to. My defiance, as they perceived it, only prompted them further into believing that they should section me. This was the wall I was up against. If I played their game in order to prove to them that I was sane it would kill me. If I protected my body I would be put away. There was no way out.

At a later date, when I was able to read through my medical notes myself, alongside my anorexia nervosa diagnosis I found an interesting test result. During the hospital's inquest into my stomach troubles, I had tested positive for faecal calprotectin. The normal range for this is 0-50 mg/kg. My level was 210 mg/kg. Underneath the visibly high result was typed, 'This indicates gastrointestinal inflammation, suggest referral to gastroenterology.'

Upon researching what the elevated result meant I found that, interestingly enough, it pointed toward inflammatory bowel diseases including ulcerative colitis, Crohn's disease, and colitis. Besides this, there had been one more abnormal test result. After looking into it further I discovered that it indicated chronic inflammation and acute and chronic infection.

The fact that both of these results had been ignored is very sad to me as it can only mean one of two things: Either, the doctors had overlooked the abnormalities on purpose so that they would not have to acknowledge their erroneous assumptions and negligence in care or they were so incompetent in their profession that they had all missed them. This 'mistake' had allowed me to edge ever nearer to death when I could have instead been provided with appropriate medical treatment. The respect and common decency that would have come from them recognising my physical condition would have been an added bonus.

As a serious illness progresses, it slowly strips away a person's sense of autonomy, self-respect and right to privacy. So much of that had already been taken away from me before I entered the hospital. Because of the immense amount of added strain that I was now being made to withstand, I no longer had the ability to use the toilet without someone else's complete assistance. The experience of having a nurse hold me steady on a commode while I relieved myself was what took away the last scrap of dignity that I had left.

My mum would give me a quick bed bath in all of the essential places every few days. I felt dirty all of the time but there was nothing I could do about it. This dilemma is a perfect representation of how everything in my life had become. Either consent to the intolerable agony of bathing or live with the feeling of being filthy. The latter was actually preferable to me than the pain that I would have to tolerate in order to be washed.

I can imagine how easy it would be for someone who has never experienced this level of debilitation to think, 'Just get through it, deal with the discomfort and then you can feel clean'. I am pretty sure that I could have braved the minutes that it took for my mum to bathe me if that was all there was to it. But it was the harsh repercussions that would last anywhere from hours to days that I dreaded more than anything.

Despite my severe reaction to noise, halfway through my stay I was put into a communal room filled with other patients. Before arriving there, I assumed that it would be of paramount importance to keep these areas quiet and calm at all times possible. This was certainly not the case in my room. Although I wore my ear defenders, the amount of noise that reached my ears was devastating to me.

Patients that weren't as ill were talking loudly on their phones or chatting and laughing with nurses as they walked by. One of them was even singing flamboyantly off and on throughout the days that I was there. The staff spoke loudly with them, called out information to each other across the large room and even shouted out food orders at meal times. The cleaners came in and banged about every day. The worst period was during visiting hours when the room would become full with family and friends, all talking at the same time as each other. Small children were even allowed to run around. I wasn't the only one who was finding it difficult to cope with the commotion. Other patients within the room were complaining that they couldn't bear the noise level.

Almost as soon as I had arrived at the new space, I noticed that one of the nurses on duty had a bit of a mean streak. I often heard her purposely provoking other frail patients and so made it a point to avoid her. When I needed something, I would wait until she had left the vicinity before asking for help from another member of staff. But on one occasion I had to go to the toilet while she was the only nurse nearby. I waited and waited but no one else came. In the end I realised that she was going to have to be the one I asked.

When the lady came near, I said 'toilet'. She replied in the kind of voice that would be used on a toddler, 'No, use your words. We need you to say a complete sentence now. Tell me what you need.' This was only the beginning. I unwillingly replied, 'I….need….the….toilet' with all of the strength I could muster. She brought the commode into my area and put it near my bed. It was common knowledge amongst the staff that I could not get out without assistance. For that reason, every other nurse had helped me automatically but with her it was different. I was aware that the recovery time I was to face would increase for every additional word I had to say. Because of this, I remained quiet in my bed, praying that she would act.

After waiting for what seemed like an eternity, I realised that there was no way around it. I said the word 'help', but this was not going to work either. I tried repeating the word a couple of times, becoming more ill by the second. It felt like a showdown. Who was going to break first? Every time she spoke it was excruciating to me. All she did was to keep repeating, 'I told you that the commode is next to the bed. I don't know what you need. Please tell me by using your words.' This went on for a couple of minutes until finally I was lifted onto it.

Like I mentioned previously, I did not have the strength to be able to hold myself up while sitting. I had to lay with my head and arms on the bed in front of me. Even this position was extremely difficult for me to maintain. Unfortunately, the nurse had the toilet paper. Once I had finished, I held out my hand for the roll but again was met with the same response. I had to use my words in order to be allowed any of this precious commodity.

The physical energy that was being drained out of my body in order to remain on the commode had depleted me so thoroughly that I didn't know how to do one more thing. I couldn't bear what she was putting me through. I stammered out the words 'toilet paper'. She replied in her baby voice, 'What do you need? Tell me again.'

By this point I was using every ounce of my strength not to fall off my seat. I felt like I was going to pass out. I whispered again in my weakened voice, 'toilet paper'. She asked, 'Which toilet paper do you need, this one or this one?' as she held up a box of tissues and then the toilet paper. I pointed to the obvious answer. But again, I was met with the singsong voice stating that I must use my words, or she could not help me.

I knew that I would collapse any second if she did not give me the goddamn loo roll and so I said to her with as much venom as I could muster, 'Give... Me... the FUCKING Toilet Paper.' She replied all calmly in her sweet sickly tone, 'Now there's no need to get all nasty about it. Ask me politely.' If I could have stood up at that moment and walked over to the other side of that bed, I would have strangled her, so I suppose it was lucky for her that I was presently dying of starvation. After experiencing that level of cruelty, all I wanted to do was to curl up in my own bed with the covers over my head and remain there until this nightmare was over.

That same day my parents were allowed to visit me. As soon as they were at my bedside, I told them what had been happening in as few words as possible. I implored them to find a way for me to be discharged from the hospital. Unbeknownst to me, on their way in, my parents had met another mother who was also visiting her daughter in the same ward. The woman told them that during an earlier time in her life she too had become bedridden with ME, describing her symptoms as almost identical to my own. She urged my parents to find a way to remove me from the hospital as quickly as possible, 'otherwise', she warned, 'they will kill her'.

Upon hearing my pleas, their protective parent power kicked in. They spoke angrily with the head nurse and demanded that I be discharged at once. Miraculously, at this time, all of my usual doctors were not around. In their place there was only a young junior doctor who had been assigned to see over my case.

Less than 24 hours before this, my stomach had surprisingly been able to manage about two thirds of a meal replacement drink over the course of the day. I found this new ability very peculiar but was, nevertheless, extremely grateful for it. That drink ended up being beneficial to me in more ways than one as it was to play a key role in setting me free. When the junior doctor saw the new development in my notes, he told my parents that there was absolutely no reason why I couldn't discharge myself if I wanted to. All I needed to do was sign a document stating that I wanted to leave, despite doctors' recommendations.

To this day I have no idea if my medical team had opted not to share that piece of information with us or if the junior doctor simply had no idea what he was doing. None of us stopped to argue the point. I managed to use a pen to scribble some sort of mark on the form faster than you could say 'Emancipation'. After ten days spent in that hell hole, I was released at long last.

My mum wheeled me out of the hospital as fast as her legs could carry her to where my dad was waiting in the car just outside. I was placed in my bed shortly thereafter. I can remember the first moment that I lay down as the silence and darkness enveloped my weary body. A sense of relief washed over me like I have never felt before or since. I let out a massive groan as it sunk in that I was in the safety and protection of my own room. I was finally home after the most terrifying experience of my life.

Not long after, my mum decided, with my consent, to set up a lasting power of attorney. This was done so that we would never again be as defenceless as we had been in that hospital. If doctors ever did declare that I was incapable of making my own decisions, my mother would be the person given control over my well-being; the person who understood my condition the best and would listen to my wishes exclusively. If this happened, I would, in effect, be able to continue to govern my own life.

Being in possession of that legal document provided me with some sort of reassurance. Regardless of this, the panic that I had felt during that hospital stay would not subside. I was so grateful to be home yet was left with an intense fear that the powers that be could come into my room at any moment and take me back. I was deathly afraid that the doctors would discover that I had not been discharged properly and would still be able to demand that I be given that mental health assessment. I lived day in and day out with these frightening and unabating thoughts.

It is common knowledge amongst the ME community that hospitals and doctors in general have no clue what they are doing when it comes to providing them with proper treatment and care. I understand that medical professionals cannot keep abreast of every illness in the world. Because of this, I could forgive them of their erroneous behaviour if they had still afforded me the level of respect and decency that every human being deserves. However, their lack of knowledge does not give them the right to assume that a mental illness is to blame when no proof of one exists or to treat someone so badly based upon that assumption. Healthcare providers have an obligation to listen to their patients and make every effort to meet them where they are at. It is the very least that they can do.

This has been the hardest chapter for me to relive. The stifling feelings of oppression and total disregard that I experienced while under the hospital staff's 'care' was far more traumatising to me than all of the severe physical suffering that I endured during that same timespan. Having to face their unrelenting inhumanity was utterly soul-destroying.

CHAPTER 8
TREES AND GRASS AND CARS AND PEOPLE

The week I spent in hospital was the only timespan during my entire illness where the search for my cure had to be put on hold, strictly out of necessity. Even in the weeks before that, as I had been wasting away in my bed, my mum had been frantically searching to find some new avenue for me. However, because of the precarious state I was in, there seemed to be nothing left that I could participate in. The day clinic was only a two-minute car ride away from the house and yet my body no longer had the small amount of energy that was required to travel in and out each day. My doctor was not licensed to make home visits and so it became impossible for me to be reinstated as her patient. I needed something that I could do from home.

Just before my admittance into hospital, my mum happened to have a conversation with another patient in the clinic who had been given the same diagnosis as my own. She wasn't in as dire a state as I but had nevertheless been heavily debilitated by Lyme disease and her many co-infections. The lady said that she was using a new and alternative treatment that was actually having positive results.

That night, my mum passed the information on to me in the shortened language that we had grown accustomed to. She relayed that there was a new possible treatment to try and I could stay at home while receiving it. I understood that it involved injections of a natural substance that was helping someone in a similar position as I was in: 'Treatment... Home... Shots... Natural... Working.' I decided to go for it. There was no reason for me to say no. I knew nothing more than the handful of words that had been transmitted slowly and carefully to me, but it failed to matter. The only information I needed was that there was something new to try that didn't involve leaving my bed.

It was left in the hands of the same magnanimous members of my family to determine whether they would pay for the new and unorthodox venture. I imagine that it must have been a difficult decision to make, as they had only just finished contributing the entire expense of the last unsuccessful one. How incredibly generous and kind they were, yet again, to agree to fund my next endeavour. It was another form of treatment that had not been widely accepted into standard medicine. To try it was going out on a limb, but they stepped up, regardless. My aunts and uncles held on to the belief that I could heal and remained committed in their aim to help transform this conviction into reality.

My mum researched the product and company thoroughly; reading facts, statistics and testimonials and watching videos online. The information that she received was extremely promising. The product was called GcMAF. This acronym is the name of a human protein that all of us innately have inside of us. It is a part of the immune system that fights inflammation, infections and viral and immune diseases. Over time, an unresolved pathogen can cause the protein to deplete, making it difficult for the body to heal itself. Injecting this natural substance back into it, rebuilds the depressed immune system so that it can eradicate any disease causing microorganism on its own.

The website claimed that this 'supplement', for lack of a better word, was treating many illnesses successfully including stage four cancer, autoimmune diseases, autism, Crohn's disease, hepatitis, MS, the list goes on and on. As it was a completely natural substance there were no reported side effects. The only instruction was to avoid taking anything that suppressed the immune system as this would counteract any positive changes that the protein could instigate.

When my mum contacted the company, she was informed that I needed to take a slightly different product called Goleic. The reason for this was that I was having medicine injected into my port on a regular basis to minimise the risk of blood clots. Unfortunately, it was one of the very few that counteracted with GcMAF. Luckily the version I was to be given worked very similarly to the original.

I received my first dose only fifteen days before entering hospital. It was given to me by small intramuscular injections which needed to be kept in the freezer. A protocol was provided that was created specifically for my situation. It took into account what was ailing me and the poor physical state that I was in. I had to have one injection every four days using a small needle. My mum performed the deed for me as, obviously, I hadn't the strength to do it myself. The small amount of pain that I experienced as the needle pierced my skin felt effortless after all of the practice I had gained during the previous year spent at the day clinic.

Every time I was given an injection I didn't wait to see if there would be an encouraging response. By this point I was so tired of feeling enthusiastic about each thing that came my way. Honestly, after all that had happened on my long and winding journey, I personally held out little hope that the attempt would work.

This was the first time that I had not become excited about a new opportunity. I decided to give it a chance simply because it would be better than doing nothing. I had no knowledge of the extensive list of serious illnesses that the product was being boasted to successfully treat but even if I had, I don't believe I would have become any more encouraged. Every other treatment I had tried thus far had possessed its own affirmations but, in my case, they had all ended in failure.

The information that was provided claimed that my strengthening immune system would begin to fight any dormant viruses and bacteria that currently existed within my body. However, my mum was warned that if they sensed the attack, it was possible for these pathogens to 'wake up' and begin to fight back. This bodily response was called an IRIS reaction. If it occurred, my symptoms would increase substantially, resulting in me feeling much worse. It was therefore necessary to increase the dose of Goleic very slowly in order to avoid such an episode.

Because of my pronounced deterioration, I had been instructed to carry out the procedure even more gradually than what was usually suggested. I began on 0.01ml. This miniscule amount was added to every second shot that I received so that I was on 0.01ml for two injections, and then moved to 0.02ml for the next eight days, and so on. At this rate, as long as the plan worked smoothly, it would take me over six months to reach my target measure of 0.25ml.

My mum was told to watch for any signs of an IRIS reaction. If one occurred, my dose would have to be lowered. It would then remain at the same level for a week or two in order to give my body time to settle down before resuming the climb, 0.01ml at a time. This meant that the painstakingly slow process could potentially drag out even longer. The company did not claim that anything positive would begin to happen before being on the full dose. I was going to have to be extremely patient over the coming months; a requirement that I knew all too well.

By the time I was admitted into hospital, I had only received four injections at a very low dose. I had been on Goleic for a mere fifteen days. The peculiar thing was that when making the difficult journey there I actually noticed something different. When I had sat up in my wheelchair to get to the ambulance and again from the vehicle into the hospital, I had noticed that I *could* sit up. Before being moved, I had automatically prepared myself for the extreme PoTS symptoms that always followed when my body was put into an upright position; that immediate urgency to lay down, as if I was going to collapse and pass out at any moment.

During the few minutes that I was in the wheelchair I had felt extremely weak from the lack of nutrients in my body and had needed to slouch down in my seat for the entire ride. However, there was no accompanying sensation that a drop in my blood pressure would have caused. Although the feeling had been unbearable, it was not nearly so drastic as it could have been. Ever since I had become bedridden, all I had witnessed was a sharp downhill trend in my health. I was bewildered by what had happened. However, at that moment I had felt no excitement because of being consumed by trying to survive the trip.

Something else abnormal had occurred upon entering the hospital. Before being assessed I had been made to lay down in a very noisy corridor for about an hour. Although I had kept my earplugs in and ear defenders on, I could still manage to hear a small level of sound; an amount that would have been deafening to me only days before. I had prepared myself for the absolute worst but to my amazement was able, with extreme difficulty, to endure the muffled noise for almost half the time before my body went into total crash mode. Comparing that to the approximately five seconds that I would have previously been able to survive the commotion, I see it as a pretty significant change.

All of the predictable and excruciating symptoms had come on in the end but that didn't change the fact that two symptoms that had plagued me for years had been drastically minimised. I began to acknowledge and contemplate these surprising new developments. I did question if they could have been a result of the new treatment but then remembered that I was on 0.02ml of the substance and had been given only four injections. Nevertheless, it seemed odd to me that as I was literally starving to death, these small random changes were simultaneously taking place.

Despite all of the anguish that I'd had to tolerate during my hospital stay, I was able to partially retain these small but significant improvements. My extreme sensitivity to sound had reached a fever pitch after not even half an hour in the loud atmosphere of the hospital hallway, and yet, during the time when I was immersed in the noisiness of the shared ward I noticed that I was coping slightly better than I had anticipated. The key word to take into consideration here is 'slightly'. It was still an absolute nightmare for me, don't get me wrong, but I could not deny that something was different. If I had been put into that ward only weeks before, I am convinced that it would have finished me off. Instead, the experience was agonising and barely sustainable but nevertheless, I survived.

Regarding my PoTS symptoms, those positive changes actually never left. After the doctor had inserted the feeding tube in my stomach, my bed was placed at a 90 degree angle for a few hours for the team to observe me. I was extremely fearful of what was going to happen, as only a few months before this, a purposely made two-inch raise to the angle of my bed in the day clinic had destroyed me. To my shock, this time there was no adverse reaction. I was so thankful for this small reprieve.

The fact that during the last 24 hours in hospital I had suddenly begun to successfully ingest a meal replacement drink had been very strange to me indeed. At the time it happened, I didn't consider that it could have been the effects of the Goleic as by then I had only been taking it for three weeks. When I got home, I very quickly began to be able to manage a couple of the gentle nutrient rich drinks a day. This was a remarkable change from only the week before. However baffling it was, I was so relieved to be able to put some nutrition back into my body after months of struggling to stay alive. Every time I had a sip of the drink, I could feel my blood sugar beginning to rise and the wooziness subsiding.

By the time I left the hospital, my stamina had weakened considerably from everything that had transpired. In spite of this, within a couple of weeks of being home I had recovered back to my normal baseline. This was another occurrence that didn't make any sense.

The progress I was witnessing didn't stop there. Touch and sight began to become slightly easier also. For over a year now my mum hadn't even been able to sit silently in the corner of my room without me feeling sheer exhaustion from both her presence and the normal small amount of fidgeting that went along with the visit. One day, about a week after I returned home, I asked my mum to lay on the bed with me. I even requested for her to put her fingers gently on my arm. I was able to withstand the trial for about a minute before she had to leave the bedroom but considered this to be a major breakthrough.

The day that I invited my mum to stay was the first time that I had been able to handle any connection with a person in years. The physical discomfort and energy depletion I had previously experienced when enduring any form of contact was so severe that I had been forced to avoid it at all costs. Evading my distressing symptoms would take full precedence as the suffering that ensued would inhibit any pleasure I could possibly receive.

My only companions for all of this time had been two pigeons that had become regular visitors, sitting on the balcony railings right outside of my window each day. They were my only source of comfort in my state of desolation. Whenever I could manage it, I would open my eyes for a brief second and focus in on their unwavering stare, imagining that they understood everything I was going through and were there to see me through my darkest hours.

As the weeks went by, I began to see other advancements quickly taking place. So much so, that within only a few weeks after coming out of hospital and six weeks on Goleic, I was able to venture out into the living room, lay down on the sofa and have a small one-sided conversation!!! To talk, and to move, and to see a sight other than the four walls I had been entombed in for the last three years was incredible. The fact that it was happening felt inconceivable to me, and yet it was!

Let's back up a moment.

During this time, I could open my eyes and remove my eye mask, although I had to keep my ear defenders on. The conversation would be intermittent within the five minutes that I could manage to stay in the living room. I was able to speak much easier than to listen as the comprehension it took to concentrate was still too much for me to handle. Afterwards, I would collapse for the rest of the day. And yet it was five whole minutes!

I found that the best time for my escapades was always about midway through the afternoon as this was when my body would reach its strongest point. I would wait in anticipation for that magical hour to come around. As soon as it did, I was out of my bed.

Before this, the only time I had left my cell of a room was to be transported to the clinic around the corner. But as soon as I had gotten out of bed and into my wheelchair, I had to have my eyes shut with a cover over them to protect me from the light and movement that would inevitably drain me of every bit of my energy. I didn't open my eyes once, not even for a second. For almost three years I never saw a thing beyond the limited space of my bedroom. And even that I only viewed during the rare moments when I had enough stamina.

After the extensive time that I had spent in isolation, I had almost completely forgotten about the world. At one point I tried to visualise what was outside of my room. I thought, 'I know there are trees…and cars…and grass…and people' but beyond that I just couldn't remember. I couldn't even recall any of the details that made up the trees and cars and people, I simply knew that those objects did exist.

I could no longer recollect any pleasures such as beauty, kindness, love, laughter and happiness. I had forgotten about all of the reasons that there were to live. Not being able to communicate or have any other connection to the world at large such as through TV or books definitely had a role to play in this loss of memory. Because of the endless monotony of it all, my perception of what constituted life had slowly but surely evaporated.

The first time that I saw out of the confines of my own room it felt utterly surreal. To become aware of there being something else in the world other than my miniscule existence was mind-blowing. I was reminded of texture, colour, depth, a reality made of matter and motion. To be able to look into someone else's eyes and see them looking back into my own was inexplicably gratifying. Each day I would be waiting on the edge of my seat, so to speak, for that momentary period of time, despite knowing that I would have to spend the rest of the evening in agony while my body attempted to recover.

Regardless of the inevitable repercussions, I realised how truly phenomenal those five minutes were. I spent a lot of this precious time quietly looking around the room, noticing each and every ornament, shelf, appliance and cupboard. I would speak very slowly and take rests in between sentences until I could feel my energy begin to slip. I would then, very begrudgingly, be escorted back into the dark abyss that was my room.

It was a difficult thing to do, knowing that once I returned to my bed, I would merely exist for another 24 hours. All of the time that I had had no sense of what life could be like, it had been, in some ways, easier than when I was actually given a small fraction of it back. The taste made me hunger for more and it became even harder to watch the minutes of the clock ticking by until I could extricate myself from my small confines. Each morning I would wake up and focus solely on that part of the day.

Once I was able to open my eyes and move around, I became aware of the sorry state that I was in. Although my hair was still very long, the near starvation had reduced its thickness to only about a third of what it used to be. My heart would break every time I caught a glimpse or a feel of it. One afternoon I asked my mum for some scissors. That day I used my living room energy to cut my hair instead. I grabbed it as best as I could while in the laying down position, lacing my fingers around the tangled mats and chopped my way through the thin ponytail that was left, bursting into tears immediately afterwards.

Up until this point, I had not been able to learn anything about the supplement myself. Now, during the magical five minutes per day, my mum would gradually fill me in on what it was and how it worked. After all of the positive changes that had occurred, I began to wonder if this could possibly be the answer that I had been searching for, but I didn't become overexcited.

My mum began to talk to me about when I was going to be well only a few days after I was able to listen. The level of enthusiasm she felt spilled out of her whenever I was in her presence. For the first time, I wouldn't allow her to speak positively about my new venture. Whenever she began, I would stop her in her tracks and say, 'Please just let me wait and see. Let's not project into the future. I just can't take the disappointment if it doesn't work.'

I was aware that having faith would give the treatment a higher chance of working, but I had simply been through too much and was too emotionally drained to let myself get carried away. I would tell my mum how I was feeling each day and share with her any improvements that I could report. We would stick with that and speak no further about the injections or our hopes for them.

I had started the supplement at a crucial time as upon entering my system, it had almost immediately begun to heal my stomach complaints. This was the affliction that had the power to determine whether I lived or died. All the others could wait. Within a week of coming out of hospital I was able to switch from my diet of meal replacement drinks to a small amount of bland food. It really was a miracle.

At first, all I could digest was blended chicken and rice but over the next few weeks the amount and variety expanded until I was able to cover all five food groups. It couldn't exactly be deemed a normal diet, but it was a large step for me in the right direction, nevertheless. Once my strength improved, I was able to use the commode on my own again, giving me a sense of some autonomy. The agonising pain of starvation and utter depletion that I had endured for so many months had come to an end.

Although I was immensely grateful for this life changing improvement, another condition had moved in to take its place. For some unexplained reason, I was now having to eat around the clock.

If I didn't, I would start to feel faint. Rather than my body preventing me from eating anything, it was now forcing me to eat huge meals with a high protein and fat content every couple of hours. I went from one extreme to the other.

The fact that I was impelled to eat when I wasn't even hungry felt horrible and also caused me to gain a large amount of weight. I wished I could simply eat the foods that I fancied when I was ready for them. But beggars can't be choosers I suppose. All I could fathom was that, after my body had experienced starvation, either my ability to absorb nutrients had worsened drastically or my hypoglycaemia had heightened. I will never know what really transpired but the symptoms were awful. Immediately after eating was the only point that I felt relief. As the time ticked by, I could sense the wooziness and feelings of depletion coming on. When I could stand it no longer my mum would come in with another gigantic plate of food.

Despite this setback, I continued to witness more improvements. Not long after I had begun the injections, the severe pain in my elbow joints completely disappeared. I had been waking up with that throbbing sensation every night for years. A little while later, the incessant ache that I had felt in both of my hips also vanished. I had always assumed that the uncomfortable symptom had been nothing more than a by-product of spending all my time in a laying down position. With this new development it became obvious that my theory had not been true.

After only a couple of months of being on Goleic my breathlessness had been reduced by about two thirds. Before attending the day clinic no doctor had been able to identify what the problem was or why it had been occurring. Even once I had obtained the much-appreciated test results clearly explaining my CO_2 imbalance, I was still unable to be treated successfully.

In order to picture how it had felt for me I would now like you, if you are healthy, to spend an entire minute taking in as small breaths as is possible, pausing for about three seconds in between each of them. This exercise will give you an impression of what I had been experiencing. After living with those devastating symptoms around the clock for so many years I had forgotten what it was like not to have them. It now felt wonderful to be able to fill my lungs with air and feel somewhat at ease with every breath I took.

At the same time as I was acknowledging each of these positive changes, I waited on tenterhooks for my energy, stamina, exploding headaches, cognition problems and sensory sensitivities to subside. These were my main symptoms; the ones that kept me feeling so desperately ill and made it impossible for me to leave my room more than once a day. After living for years with zero, five minutes of pleasure was a definite plus, but it gave me nowhere near enough stimulation to feel any sense of fulfilment. It was the other 1,435 minutes that made up each 24 hour period that I didn't know how to cope with.

During the first month of taking Goleic, within minutes of receiving each injection I had experienced a small decrease in my malaise and fatigue levels. However, that sensation had been fleeting. It would usually last for about half an hour or, if I was lucky, continue for a bit longer than that but was always completely gone by the time I woke up the next morning. As time went on, I noticed these small but positive changes becoming more prolonged until finally they were becoming permanent. That was when the injections had begun to build upon each other and when I started to make my monumental trips into the living room.

Unfortunately, at some point, these developments had stagnated. My mum was still continuing to increase my doses of the supplement incrementally every eight days. It was very difficult for me to be patient with the painfully slow process. I always wanted to jump ahead in order to try and move things along faster. After witnessing all of the recent developments, I had begun to think that perhaps, once I was on the full dose, the real changes that I was craving would begin to happen.

About three fourths of the way through the first set of bottles, my mum realised that a mistake had been made as the number of needles she had infused with Goleic didn't add up correctly. When holding them up to the light she saw that the leftover vials had air bubbles in them. As the amount of liquid required in the vials had increased, it had become more difficult to fill them accurately. For some time now, I had received less of the protein than was recommended for me in order to reach the target amount.

Although this discovery was incredibly frustrating, it also rekindled my hope. Maybe once I began to receive the injections at the proper increment, the progress I had made early on would resume itself. It now made perfect sense to both of us why so many of my symptoms had been utterly transformed at the beginning of treatment but, as of late, had begun to plateau. The handful of needles that were left had been frozen and so could not be changed but I held onto the knowledge that my mum would soon be filling the new vials with the right amount of liquid.

But only three months after I began my treatment, all production of Goleic and GcMAF was suspended within the entire country. The MHRA (the body that regulates medicines within the UK) had carried out an unannounced inspection on the laboratory and claimed that it did not meet standards of good manufacturing. The regulating body sent the product off to be tested for sterility in a government lab. This was carried out regardless of the fact that the company itself already had its merchandise approved nine times by a government laboratory.

The problem with this natural immunity-boosting product was that it was actually working. It's difficult to imagine any billion-dollar pharmaceutical companies accepting a form of thriving competition in the market. No matter if permitting these other treatments to coexist could result in many serious illnesses being ameliorated or even eradicated, giving many people who previously had no hope the chance to live full and happy lives. Interestingly enough, some of these pharmaceutical companies actually funded the MHRA. This regulating body had, in the past, been accused of concentrating its efforts on keeping drug companies happy rather than focusing on the interests of the public at large.

This unwarranted halt in production meant that, for all of the recipients of GcMAF and Goleic, treatment was forced to come to an abrupt halt. I only had a few weeks of injections left in the freezer when we found out this dismaying news. Each time my mum got another one out, I was reminded of the ever-dwindling number. All we could both do was pray that by the time I was given my last dose, the company would be back in business again.

Sadly, our prayers went unanswered. The moment that the last vial was injected into my muscle, I knew that it was over. Even if production had been allowed to restart the next day, the product could not have been shipped to me fast enough to keep it from disrupting my sensitively orchestrated regime. I had finally found something that was making a difference and it had been taken away from me. I felt anger towards everyone responsible for ceasing production but also towards the universe in general. From my bleak perspective, it was clearly working against me. No matter what I tried or what I did, there was always a reason why I wasn't able to attain that which I so desperately needed.

From the moment we were alerted that the suppliers had been shut down, my mum and I went into a state of panic. I had no idea what was going to happen. Would I ever get the chance to resume the injections? Was this it forever? Because of these ruthless actions put in place by the authorities, I was yet again, left with no form of treatment and no hope. I felt thoroughly disheartened and, naturally, sank even deeper into depression. It was becoming very hard for me to believe that I would ever be well again. My mum began to frantically hunt for some other strategy in order to procure the invaluable protein.

All the while, my body was being deprived of the one substance that was actually beginning to strengthen it. Because of this, my symptoms of post-exertional malaise, sensory sensitivities and brain fatigue rapidly reverted back to where they had been before I ever started. My magical five minutes had become out of the question for me once again. Being unable to leave my room was an especially distressing position to regress back to. I had nothing left to look forward to, no break from my endless torture. Instead, my days stretched out limitlessly. Minute after minute, hour after hour, I would watch the time slip by. I yearned for the clock to go faster, for the seconds to speed up, but my wish was never granted.

After searching tirelessly, my mum eventually found out that Goleic and GcMAF were still able to be sold and distributed within the rest of Europe. They were both also legal to bring into England as long as the purchaser had already bought and paid for the product in another country. All we needed was an address somewhere within Europe to send it to. As luck would have it, my father owned a house in Spain. The universe had decided to open its doors for me after all. We had the supplement shipped to my dad's place as quickly as possible. He then made the journey to pick it up and bring it home to me. After six weeks without an injection, I was able to resume treatment once again.

This arrangement was to continue for quite some time. Every three months my father made a special trip to Spain so that I could continue to take what we identified as the only thing left with the potential to make me well. The procedure was extremely time sensitive since the protein had to be kept refrigerated or frozen. The teeny tiny bottles were treated like gold. They were sealed within special packaging and sent to a neighbour in case my father's flight was delayed. This left no chance of the parcel remaining outside of a vacant house in the hot, Spanish sun. They were then whisked back to England as fast as possible. Once he arrived in the country, my dad would bomb down the motorway to us so that the bottles could be placed in our freezer within the mandatory time frame.

We were on the edge of our seats every time the operation was carried out, wondering whether the precious cargo would make it back in one piece. My dad would always wait until right before I ran out, God love him, which made the ordeal that much hairier for us to live through. If any part of the manoeuvre had failed; if the neighbour had not been at home to receive the parcel when it came, if airport security decided to take the bottles out of their special refrigerated packaging or not allow them through at all, if my dad's flight was cancelled, if there was a delay on the motorway on the way down, I would have had to spend weeks without the injections and risk my health deteriorating even further. As is always the case with my father, the mission went without a hitch on every single occasion. The bottles arrived within the time I needed them to for the entire length of my treatment, and for that I am eternally grateful to him.

After waiting fretfully for what seemed like a lifetime, I was finally back on my envisioned path to success. It hadn't even been two months since I had the last injection but during that time so much had changed for the worse. Nevertheless, I felt optimistic that with the correct dosage my improvements would soon resume. I expected that I would be given back my five minutes in the living room quite quickly and would then be able to build upon that time as my body slowly but surely made its way to recovery.

In order to restart the supplement I had to begin at a slightly lower dose than my last injection since my body had now grown accustomed to being without it. It was frustrating to say the least, but I accepted that I had to do things the right way if I wanted the chance to be well. I received the protein every four days, patiently anticipating the time when my lasting symptoms would again begin to diminish. However, reality didn't pan out that way. I kept having my injections, upping the dose when I was supposed to, but nothing was changing. My energy and stamina weren't increasing, and my post-exertional malaise stayed at the same intensity I had experienced before commencing the treatment.

In contrast, my breathlessness, joint pain, stomach and blood pressure issues seemed to have permanently improved. Of course, the dampening of these afflictions was advantageous to me but honestly, they were just a drop in the ocean compared to what I was still contending with. The most debilitating part of my condition and that which prevented me from leaving my bed had regressed right back to before I had ever taken Goleic.

I was never again able to resume my magical five minutes in the living room. At first, I wondered if maybe the problem was in my imagination, maybe I was stronger than I thought. But after a few unsuccessful trials of leaving my bed, I realised that it was simply no longer possible. The small reprieve that I had been given from entering a room other than my own, looking into another human being's eyes and expressing myself for a short amount of time had vanished into thin air.

All of the enthusiasm that I felt for the supplement quickly shrivelled up. I couldn't understand why it wasn't working as it had the first time around. After some contemplation, I reasoned that it must have been the involuntary break that I had taken. A doctor later explained to my mum that at the beginning, a new treatment is startling to the illness it attacks. Therefore, it is able to assume the upper hand more easily. However, when there has been an interruption, the disease is given time to prepare itself; acquiring the necessary power to fight back more fervently when the remedy is resumed.

I was furious with the pharmaceutical companies but also with the government officials for becoming involved in what some people deemed as a deceptive collaboration, done simply to line their pockets. This was my life that they were playing with, my chance to get better. What's more, I wasn't the only person to be affected. So many other unfortunate individuals were now in a similar situation to mine, many of which hadn't the means to buy the product in another European country. How could the people from those greedy corporations be so blind not to see that a human life led with freedom from suffering was more important than all of their stacks of money?

It could be said that compared to some I was lucky because my condition was not fatal. But to me my fate was becoming one that was much worse than death. There was no part of me that felt alive anymore. The only thing that kept me going through this dark and treacherous time was to think that the protein would eventually kick back in. It became the only shred of hope that I had left to hold onto.

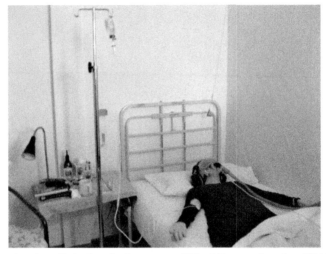

In the day clinic, hooked up to an IV while wearing the CPAP mask, eye mask and industrial strength ear defenders.

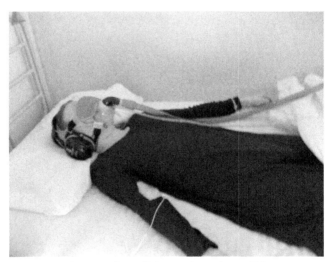

No sound, no light, no breath, no life.

My mother and I, two years before I became ill.

LYME DISEASE SYMPTOMS
EARLY LYME' -vs- CHRONIC LYME"

Fatigue 76%	Fatigue 79%
Headache 70%	Joint Pain 70%
Rash <70%	Muscle Pain 69%
Fever 60%	Other Pain 66%
Sweats 60%	Sleep Issues 66%
Chills 60%	Cognitive 66%
Muscle Pain 54%	Neuropathy 61%
Joint Pain 48%	Depression 62%
Neck Pain 46%	Heart Related 31%
Sleep Issues 41%	Headaches 50%

'(Aucott 2013) ''(Johnson 2014. Moderate to very severe symptoms)
Estimates of rash rates range from 25-80% http://tinyurl.com/kfvu8yt

Difference between the early and chronic stages of Lyme.

PRÄVENTIVE LABORDIAGNOSTIK
UND MEHR ● ●

Laboratory Jochen Hüter · Hammfelddamm 6 · 41460 Neuss · Germany

Hammfelddamm 6 · 41460 Neuss · Germany
Tel (++49) 21 31 - 12 59 69-0
Fax (++49) 21 31 - 12 59 69-69

Printed: 24.04.2014 10:04 am
Page: 1

Final Report			Order Number 0051493 - date of receipt 17.04.2014

Patients Name		Date of Birth	Gender
Steadman, Carly		08.11.1982	female

Test	Result	Unit	Reference Value
Clinical / Anamnestic data			
Anamnesis	none		
MELISA - Lyme Borreliosis - Borrelia afzelii p41-Antigen Internal Fragment			
p41 IF afzelii	**1.38**	SI	< 3
p41 IF afz. 2	**1.61**	SI	< 3
p41 IF afz. 3	**1.41**	SI	< 3
Morphology	**negative**		negative
MELISA - Lyme Borreliosis - Borrelia garinii p41-Antigen Internal Fragment			
p41 IF gar	**1.05**	SI	< 3
p41 IF gar 2	**2.13**	SI	< 3
p41 IF gar 3	**(3.47)** +	SI	< 3
Morphology	**positive**		negative
MELISA - Lyme Borreliosis - Borrelia burgdorferi senso stricto p41-Antigen Internal Fragment			
p41 IF ses	**0.84**	SI	< 3
p41 IF ses 2	**0.78**	SI	< 3
p41 IF ses 3	**0.77**	SI	< 3
Morphology	**negative**		negative
MELISA - Lyme Borreliosis - Borrelia Mix of OspA/VlsE of garinii, afzelii, s. stricto			
Peptide mix	**1.36**	SI	< 3
Peptide mix 2	**1.12**	SI	< 3
Peptide mix 3	**1.08**	SI	< 3
Morphology	**negative**		negative
MELISA - Lyme Borreliosis - Borrelia full Antigen lysate of B. burgdorferi sensu stricto			
Full antigen	**(3.24)** +	SI	< 3
Full antigen 2	**1.44**	SI	< 3
Full antigen 3	**1.31**	SI	< 3
Morphology	**positive**		negative

Positive reaction to Borrelia garinii p41 antigen (internal fragment, recombinant) and Borrelia burgdorferi
sensu stricto (full antigen), indicating an active lyme borreliosis.

Sincere regards
Jochen Hüter

MELISA Lyme test results. Specificity of this form of test is 97%
meaning that only 3% of all positive results are ever false positive.

Colchester Hospital University **NHS**
NHS Foundation Trust

Physiotherapy Department
Gainsborough Wing
Colchester General Hospital
Turner Road
Colchester
CO4 5JL

Tel: 01206 742530

10th July, 2008

RECEIVED 14 JUL 2008

Dear Dr ▬

Re: **Miss Carly Steadman dob: 08.11.1982**

The enclosed referral details for the above patient eventually arrived on my desk at the Physiotherapy Department, Colchester Hospital University NHS Foundation Trust. I also work part-time at the Colchester CFS/ME Clinic, as a physiotherapist on the team at the PCC.

This afternoon, my secretary and I took Carly's referral and results to Dr Skelly, Endrocrinologist. He felt that Carly's EBV was now in the convalescent phase, and recommended that you contact Microbiology to confirm whether Carly is still actively infected with EBV, before referring again for assessment at the Colchester CFS/ME Clinic, through Southend University Hospital. Unfortunately, there is no funding for domiciliary visits at present, so Carly would need to be well enough to travel into Colchester, for assessment and a subsequent treatment, after which telephone consultations are a possibility.

For your information I have enclosed details of Dr Martin Lerner's work in the USA with long courses of specific antiviral therapy in patients with chronic EBV infections.

If any of the above is not helpful, a referral to a named Consultant General Physician at Colchester Hospital, may be beneficial, or to an Infectious Diseases Specialist elsewhere.

Yours sincerely,

Specialist Physiotherapist
Chronic Fatigue Syndrome/ME

TU wrote 15/7

One of the misplaced letters that had been suggesting an
underlying infection, written less than a year into my illness.

CHAPTER 9

ONE AWAKENED DREAM

I lay in my bed 24 hours a day, completely still, with no aspect of outside life entering my tiny little world. I was devoid of touch, sound, daylight or any sight other than the occasional glimpse of my darkened room. Every so often I would muster up the energy to open my eyes in order to provide myself with the realisation that I was in my body, I was still human, I was alive.

My suffering had become so severe by this time that I didn't know where to put myself, figuratively speaking. I was completely trapped inside my own body, restricted from making any movement, imprisoned within a self-imposed straight jacket. Unfortunately, this restriction had become essential to me as without it the consequences would have been horrendous.

This entombment was a physical representation of the fundamental situation that I found myself in. I didn't get better. I didn't die. There was no way out for me, no chance of finding relief. I felt such a profound sense of panic. I pleaded to the universe to be sent someone who could help me as I couldn't do it on my own. But no one else could either. Time after time I had built my hopes up on others only to have them come crashing down around me.

I was aware of the utter emptiness now. I couldn't even cry out to express the severe mental and physical pain that I was living in. My body was submerged deep under murky waters but no matter how much I thrashed around, there was no coming back up for air. The darkness had engulfed and swallowed me whole.

My encompassing isolation was beyond what I could cope with. The utter lack of any form of communication or opportunity for self-expression was slowly eating away at me. I was experiencing the most harrowing moments of my life and yet could not tell anyone about them. What made this even more frightening was that there was no end in sight to my very real mental torture.

I had to find a tactic to keep my then wavering sanity from slipping away. In the silence of the room, I began to create a whole new life for myself that existed in my mind's eye. The diversion would last for the entirety of the day (as much as the painful pressure in my head would allow me to think). I pictured everything in great detail so that my fabricated world would feel as real as possible to me. It gave me so much pleasure to envision seemingly mundane scenarios and spend my day within them. I visited with my family, friends and pets, travelled both to familiar places and to those I had never been, relived past events the way I wished they had gone and future events the way I wished they could be.

After months of practice my imagination became highly trained. Whenever I made the effort, I could connect with and disappear into the other world almost immediately. I became so absorbed that I never got distracted by random thoughts as I would if I attempted to do the same thing now. My focus remained upon the imaginary scenario I had planned for the day. I could disappear for chunks of time before having to rest my mind by putting it into a sort of meditative state until the pressure subsided. And then it was back to my constructed existence.

I became completely immersed in the stories that I created for myself. Sometimes I would spend days on one singular scenario so that by the time I got to the end of the story I felt real connections to the people and places I had imagined. It was the only solace I had, the only way to escape the harshness of the real world and so I gave myself over to it willingly each and every day. I could create a new adventure whenever I wanted, taking things slowly and experiencing the events as I would if I was truly living them. The details became so vivid that I almost felt like I was really sensing them. I would see the colours, smell the smells and feel the touch against my skin.

Because of being totally deprived of pleasure for so long, these imaginary experiences became more tangible to me than my physical existence. In other words, my imagination became more real than my reality. It wasn't that I became confused about which was which but rather that I lost myself so deeply and spent so much more time there that when I momentarily came back to the real world, what remained paled in comparison to the intensity of what I had invented. As a result, all I wanted to do was disappear back into my thoughts. The days became one awakened dream. The creative part of my mind was being stimulated so often that my innovativeness even spilled over into my dreams. I would often wake in the morning with a memory of a beautiful song my subconscious mind had invented during the night (an ability that was entirely new to me).

From the outside it could appear that by disappearing all the time I was giving up but, in fact, the opposite was true. This form of distraction was a coping mechanism that I had managed to find in order to pass the days until either the injections began to work again or some other new idea was born. I still believed that there was an answer waiting for me. If I could just find the right treatment, if the right person came along, I could be well. All I needed to do was to figure out how to attack the pathogens that were residing inside my body and I would then be able to heal, simple as that.

But it wasn't as simple as that. Because of the severity of my situation, my chances of receiving any form of help had now become slim. After a few months of continuing to inject Goleic and seeing no improvement, a family member told us about a prominent specialist in infectious diseases who was based locally and willing to make home visits. He was accustomed to working with patients that presented with the type of diseases that were plaguing me. In my mind, a new doctor equalled a fresh pair of eyes. I held out hope for him to devise an innovative plan or suggest some new form of treatment that I had yet to try.

During his initial visit the physician studied my positive test results and all of my medical notes very intently, determined not to leave any stone unturned. He read through the thorough symptom questionnaires that I had previously filled out for the local day clinic. He also listened earnestly when my mum provided additional details about my medical history and how I was currently feeling.

Based upon all of this information and his own personal medical examination, the doctor had no doubt that I had Lyme disease. He diagnosed me for the second time and said that his decision had been extremely clear. He had seen many cases similar to mine during his extensive career. In contrast to my last doctor, he agreed with the traditional medical view, that after being infected with Lyme disease for two years antibiotics would not be able to work. He claimed that there was no hope for me now. My body was in too weak a state and because of this there was no turning it back.

The specialist went on to explain that the disease was still residing in my body, having converted into a dormant state. After all of these years it could not be active anymore. Consequently, all of my remaining symptoms were the resulting permanent damage. Upon hearing this statement my mum pointed out all of the positive changes that the Goleic had initially caused. The doctor dismissed them saying that they had been manufactured by my mind. His explanation was that my faith in the new treatment had created these temporary improvements. It had not been possible for my body to keep up with all that I had contrived. This was why they had passed within such a short span of time.

I knew that his words could not be true. In all of the years that I had been striving to be well, I had held out hope and belief in each and every treatment that I tried. So much so, that I would actually start to plan what I was going to do with my life once I became healthy. Every time that I began a new endeavour I was convinced that it would be the one to cure me. Yet no amount of optimism had ever helped.

The Goleic had been the first treatment that I hadn't put my heart into as by this time the torture of being let down had become much too painful for me. Nevertheless, this was the one that my body had responded to. In my mind, that was proof enough that the changes that had occurred could not be a result of my expectations and hence, neither could my symptoms be permanent damage. Regardless, the doctor was adamant about his interpretation. He told my mum that we had to accept the fact that I would never recover.

Shortly after making this grave statement, the physician shared two interesting pieces of information with my mother. The first was an intriguing story about one of his own patients. In the many years that he had worked in his vocation, he had seen quite a few extreme cases, one of which was a young girl who was suffering with severe brain damage. She had brain scans showing that her condition was permanent and was confined to a wheelchair.

One day, the girl's mother was taking her out for some fresh air. Just as they were nearing a pond, she was accidentally pushed over a rock, was catapulted out of her seat and landed in the freezing cold water. At the time she fell into the pond she was in a seriously ill state and yet moments later she walked out of the water completely healed. Was it the shock of the experience that had caused this monumental shift? No one, including my doctor, could ever explain how this miracle had occurred.

After relaying this story, the man went on to tell my mum about an interesting and recognised phenomenon within the medical profession. Very occasionally, when someone has been as ill as I had for many years, it is possible for them to have completely healed from the illness that has been the source of their distress but at the same time remain in a state of *dis-ease*, their body ignoring the transformation. In order for it to function properly again, the body would need to be prompted. To implement this, the person would need to begin to participate in some of the normal daily activities that they carried out before the illness was present. Only then would their system recognise that it could resume a healthy level of operation.

I suppose the current specialist had followed his bleak prognosis with both of these thought-provoking accounts in order to prevent us from becoming utterly deflated. The last circumstance resonated with what I had undertaken in the day clinic more than a year before when my bed had been gradually raised and I had been asked to stand for short periods of time. Although that doctor had been hopeful, none of it had been able to help me while the infections were still rampant within my body.

When my mum had shared the physician's firmly rooted prognosis with me, I told her that I wanted to try antibiotics again. There could be nothing wrong with giving the medication one last shot as I now had no other hope left. After she had finished pleading my case many times over, the doctor finally relented. Although he would only agree to dispensing a two-week course as he couldn't see any reason for me to take them.

The medicine had to be administered using a giant needle that was inserted into the gluteal muscles. As I could no longer leave my bed, my mother was obligated to take on the role of nurse. What a trooper she was. Every day for two weeks I was flipped onto my stomach and a very long, sharp needle was inserted into each bum cheek. I never saw any improvement.

When the course of antibiotics came to an end, the physician told us that because of the extent of my immobilisation, I had exhausted all of my avenues. His next recommendation would have been to have specific tests carried out on my brain. However, he was aware that my body was in too weak of a state to go into hospital. If I attempted it at this point, I would probably die.

A specialist doctor who was highly respected and experienced within his field had told my mother directly; I should accept where I was and stop trying because nothing would ever change, it was too late for me. Nevertheless, I refused to consider his assumptions. I would

NOT accept this. As I heard his words, I became immediately emphatic; 'NO. This is not true. This is not how it's going to happen.'

Considering all of the years of failed attempts, the severity of my condition, the fact that we hadn't found any form of treatment to try in months and that a doctor was now insisting that there was no hope left, I cannot begin to fathom why I still thought this way. My mind was unambiguous though. I decided very firmly, in that moment, that I would not give in. I *would* find the answer. After hearing the doctor's words, I only became more determined.

The level of desperation that I felt now was overwhelming. I became panic-stricken and implored my mum to search harder for a way forward. However, there were no clues as to where to look next. After continuing her almost impossible hunt, she did discover one other alternative healing method. My mum begged for the treatment as she knew that this could be our last chance, but the practitioner would not come out to the house. I grew increasingly disheartened. Even if there was a cure out there, I was now in too weak of a state to receive it. The illness was making any attempts for me to become well impossible.

During her ongoing search, my mum found the names of two advanced specialist Lyme disease doctors who were based in Germany. This country happens to be considerably more advanced in the detection and treatment of the illness. As a nation, they recognise that sufferers can be successfully treated with long-term antibiotics at any stage, even years down the line. This is also where much of the extensive research into the disease occurs.

Both of the doctors my mum spoke with were aware of the naivety of the UK's approach to the disease. They were horrified upon hearing all that I had been through and how no medical professional was willing to help me now. If I had been in Germany, they said they would have gladly seen and treated me. As I couldn't even leave my bed to reach the toilet anymore, there was no way I would be travelling across Europe in the near future.

A few more months went by with absolutely no new leads. After being subjected to day after day of this painfully slow punishment, I began to consider the very real possibility that there *was* nothing left to try. Even though I am not a religious person, it was then that I began to pray. I wished with all of my might for the energies in the universe to send me the answer.

It was very peculiar but, in these moments that were entirely absent of hope, I still felt instinctually that I would be well. I was coming to the practical conclusion that there was no way that it could be true but in my heart I continued to feel differently. Why this stark contrast existed, I cannot explain. Nevertheless, I was convinced that a lifeline would be provided. I kept thinking, 'Something is going to come. If we continue to look, a solution will be found.'

Alongside becoming lost within my own beautiful imaginary scenarios, I also began to spend time envisioning my self-imposed death. It was simply another way for me to make it through each day. This activity sounds like the last thing in the world that would keep a person going. However, for me it proved quite the contrary. Visualising the release that would come with my passing provided me with a way out. If I had been unable to see an end to all of the suffering, I wouldn't have been strong enough to make it through one more hour. Picturing my death was what was keeping me alive.

I was aware that I couldn't go on like this forever. I was being tortured both mentally and physically, day after day, with not a moment of rest. I decided that I had to give myself a date. If nothing had been found by that time, I would put an end to the agony myself. Every instance that I felt as though I couldn't make it through the next five minutes I would think, 'It's only this many weeks longer.' There was now a limited time frame in which I had to survive the pain of my existence and in that awareness, I found the resilience that I needed.

As you read this you may be thinking that I wanted to die but nothing could have been further from the truth. I yearned to live and to be healthy. I would pray every day that an answer would come before the chosen date. Death was not what I wanted but a logical, planned out solution to my dilemma. It was not a decision made hastily or in an irrational state. It was weighed up and thought out thoroughly during the endless emptiness of my days.

Amongst the darkness there was *one* source of upliftment that my mind could gravitate towards. Overtime, my mum had managed to slowly impart the two inspiring stories that the specialist doctor had shared with her. Although this had been done in short form, missing out many of the details, I did not take either of them lightly. They both sparked my interest and kept me captivated during the months that I lay in wait.

Each of them seemed surreal in their own right. For my body to already be well sounded like an impossibility when I felt so gravely ill and was experiencing countless excruciating symptoms. During the passing months I had occasionally attempted to make a small movement in bed. The resulting repercussions had been so severe that I would rather have been dead than to have lived through them. How could all of that pressure build up in my head if I had nothing wrong with me? How could the rest of my already waning energy drain from my body after simply moving a hand if I was no longer ill? After much consideration, I reasoned that this circumstance could not conceivably relate to my personal situation. Even still, the idea disturbed me.

But the story that fascinated me the most was of the girl that had fallen in the water only to walk out completely healed. Upon hearing it I thought, 'Why can't I be her? What's stopping me? She was an ordinary girl. There was nothing magical about her. She had no secret powers and yet this miracle had occurred.' These thoughts ran over inside of my head. I lay there day after day, contemplating what I could do to become like her and how I would go about it.

After what seemed like an eternity spent in a pointless void, the truth finally dawned on me one day; I had been waiting in vain. There was no saviour coming to rescue me. There was no miraculous treatment. All this time I had believed there was an answer out there for me to find. But this just wasn't so. Within minutes of that realisation, I made a crucial decision; *I* was the person who had to make it happen. There was no other option for me now. I would become the girl in the pond.

CHAPTER 10
IN A WORLD OF COMPLETE SILENCE

In the moment of my decision, I felt a burst of enthusiasm. I immediately became resolute that I would not let any terrifying thoughts of what could happen enter my awareness. I called my mum into the room by using the special button that I had to alert her. When she entered, I asked for the wheelchair and said, 'I'm going out.' She looked shocked but immediately went to retrieve it, being conscious of the gargantuan effort that it had just taken for me to produce those words. With her assistance, I got into the chair and told her in no uncertain terms, 'I'm going to be the girl that fell in the pond. Take me to the park right now.'

I was taken to the car as fast as my mum could wheel me. I hadn't bathed properly in weeks and was wearing a dirty nightdress that I had been in for the same length of time. My hair was a mess; oily and cut jaggedly at all different lengths. None of it concerned me. With the help of my mum, I got into the front seat and lay back with my eyes closed and my ear defenders on, attempting to conserve as much energy as I could.

As we neared the park, I opened my eyes and was able to see the trees and grass rushing by out of the car window. The sheer magnitude of the colour blew me away. The green in the grass looked as if it was fluorescent. The trees were so incredibly beautiful that they made me cry. I couldn't believe that this was what people saw and took for granted every day of their lives. It looked like paradise to me. These words are no exaggeration.

I can remember saying to my mum, 'If there is a heaven, this is what it would look like. We have it here on Earth.' I was merely viewing an average park in the beginning of October. Just to see the leaves blowing in the trees was breath-taking. All of my senses were heightened. Once we were parked, still crying, I got into the wheelchair without taking my eyes off of our destination for one second. I looked up and gasped as I saw how vast the sky was.

My mum then began to push me gingerly towards the park. I told her to go faster as I couldn't wait to get there. I could feel my energy fading and the terrible exhaustion coming on from all of the movement and speaking that I was doing but I didn't care. I wanted to see that park, to be right amongst it and feel the warmth of the sun on my face for as long as possible. My mum became worried that

I might be cold but, in that moment, none of it was important. I just wanted as much fresh air as I could feel on my skin and breathe into my lungs.

I could hardly see all of the beauty through the tears that were, by now, streaming down my face. I had completely forgotten about this thing called 'life' that was happening beyond my four walls. It was incredible to me that people lived their day to day lives so easily and freely. I watched a teenage boy as he manoeuvred a skateboard up and down a large and elaborately formed ramp and an old man out for his slow but steady morning walk. I observed a woman throwing a ball for her Labrador and the dog having such a wonderful time running around in the dewy grass.

I couldn't get over the amount of pleasure that there was in the world. Joy had long ago been erased from my memory, not only how it felt but simply the fact that it existed. I had not witnessed or personally experienced any happiness or enjoyment whatsoever for such a long time. Watching these modest acts in all of their varied forms was mind-blowing.

Life could be so easy. I didn't understand why people chose to struggle. I knew that the details of living weren't that black and white, but I could also perceive that if a person was healthy, they had an opportunity to make their life how they wanted it to be. All of the people that I was watching in the park had their chance. Did they realise how lucky they were to possess such a gift? I didn't feel any jealousy but instead was filled with immense happiness for each person that I saw that day, although at the same time I wished with all of my heart that my life could have been different. I couldn't stop crying. These tears were of joy from witnessing the many forms of simple beauty mixed with tears of sorrow for all of the years of my life that had been wasted. In that moment I sensed the loss more strongly than ever.

My existence had been filled with misery and darkness for so long now that I had forgotten about the light. I had ceased to remember how effortless and uncomplicated life could be. As I had been given nothing to compare it to, I had slowly become unaware of the true severity of my situation. It saddened me to realise how arduously I had struggled for so many years; all of the battles I had faced, the level of debilitation I had dealt with, the severe symptoms I had endured. I was shocked by how consumed I had become by the war that was raging inside of me, how starved I was of anything but this. I was using every ounce of my strength in attempts to embody the girl that had changed her whole world within seconds. Nevertheless, I could feel that my pleas were not being met. My already excruciating symptoms had reached past that which I could withstand and I didn't know how I was going to continue to sit up.

I did not care how great the repercussions were going to be. I was determined to suck every minute that I could out of the experience. As I sat there, feeling my energy fading away, it became apparent that this was the last time that I would see the outside world, the final moment for me to feel the breeze on my face and the sun on my back, to witness other beings going about their daily lives and the last time that I would feel any sort of pleasure.

In that highly poignant moment, I hugged my mum as tight as it was possible for me to do and cried in silence as I let the seconds tick by. All the while, I kept my eyes wide open in order to watch the trees moving in the breeze and the clouds passing through the blue sky above. In the end the pain became too great and even though I never wanted to have to utter the words, I told my mum to take me home. This marked the point of no return. There was no way now that my body could ever come back from what I had put it through. It is hard for me to articulate the level of debilitation that I felt then. I had believed that I was already at rock bottom before the trip to the park but apparently with this illness it was possible to go underground.

I could no longer move my body even a centimetre without regretting the action more than anything I had ever regretted in my life. I couldn't open my eyes for a second. I couldn't take one word being spoken to me and neither could I speak one to anyone. I was officially a vegetable. I was unable to see, move, hear, or say anything. I couldn't feed myself, I couldn't be washed. Even in the stillness and the silence, the simple movement of my breathing was extremely debilitating. There really was nothing left.

After living in this dire state for seven whole days, my self-given 'expiry date' was still over four weeks away. Each day of that first week I had thought, 'I must hold on until then. Whatever level of pain I feel, I cannot give in. I *will not*.' I had always been someone who kept to my word, and this was the most important commitment I had ever made to anyone, including myself. I vowed to keep the promise that I had made. In my thoughts, there was still a chance that a cure would find me.

But five days on, I could no longer stand the immensity of the pain that I was in. I didn't even know how I was going to make it through the next two minutes, let alone a whole day or the seven days that made up each of the weeks that was left for me to face. I woke up one morning and immediately became aware that I couldn't fight any longer. The day had come.

It is of paramount importance to me to make something clear to my readers. Even on the actual day that was to mark my death, I did not want to commit the act. There was no panic or confusion in my mind that morning. The decision to put an end to my suffering was based on the fact that I knew rationally that there was nothing more to hold on to or to try. I had exhausted all avenues. My body was too ill to accept any form of treatment.

More importantly, after so many years spent in agony and distress, I needed to be released from it all. If I could have figured out any other way to do that, I would have taken it. It was the only answer for me now although I wished fervently that it wasn't so. Even on the morning that I realised that I could no longer wait, I chose to delay the event until the end of the day just in case some miracle happened upon me.

It was a peculiar situation to be in to say the least. I had always assumed that a suicidal person would be in a state of hysteria. I'm sure some people take their lives when they are feeling unstable, without thinking it through. However, there must be a great deal of instances like mine, when the decision has been considered thoroughly. I had also supposed that, at the very least, everyone in this situation *wanted* to kill themselves. I hadn't understood that there were many individuals out there just like me, who desperately desired to live but found themselves cornered into too demanding of a position with absolutely no way out.

I had come to the conclusion that, because of my limited strength and means, I was going to have to cut my wrists. I have always had an enormous phobia of blood so facing the physical action was going to be a task in itself, but it also happened to be the option requiring the least assistance. My mother would only need to place a knife on my bed. I thought up other scenarios, but they always involved too much of an outside responsibility. There had to be no possibility that my mum would end up being blamed for playing any kind of role in my plans.

After contemplating the amount of energy that it was going to take for me to do the deed, I surmised that I could manage it. I had to. I would wait until the end of the day for any miracles to present themselves and then, if none came, the plan would be executed. By using this method, I could wait until my mum had gone to sleep before I did it. However, I knew that I was going to have to share my plan with her beforehand. If she had been left in the dark, the extent of the shock and horror upon discovering my lifeless body would have been too great. I wanted her to be prepared.

My heart ached each and every time I deliberated what my mother was about to endure. She had given up her life for me. Through her unparalleled dedication she had undergone such hardship herself; continuously fighting with ignorant doctors, giving up her job in order to care for me full-time, isolating herself when coming to live near the day clinic, seeing me in distress each and every day, witnessing me almost die from starvation and now, the last hurdle; having to learn that her daughter's life would be over in less than 24 hours. And for what?

All that pain and struggle we had both been through, for it to come to this. I felt so sorry to leave her and so guilty to have to ask her for this one last favour; the biggest request that I would ever have to make, but I could think of no other way. I was also mindful of my father and the other members of my family and friends who cared about me; all of the people who would be devastated. I hoped that they would find it in their hearts to understand that the level of torment that I had been subjected to had gone beyond what I could handle.

Never in all of my wildest dreams had I believed that the forthcoming events would ever transpire. I had always been so confident that one day I would be well again. It was shocking to me that my life hadn't panned out that way. What was even more bizarre was that even though my decision was final, and my fate appeared to be sealed, I simultaneously possessed an unshakable feeling that I was not going to die. It was a very contradictory place to be in.

The thought that continuously repeated in my mind was, 'There must be a miracle coming to me today, there just must be.' I couldn't understand where this conviction was coming from, but it was there, as strong as I stand here today. As I planned all of the details out that morning it felt like I was playing a game of make-believe. I was pretending that these things would happen while in all actuality I knew that they were not to come.

When my mum came into the bedroom, I had no idea how to begin the conversation. It all felt so surreal. Whatever physical repercussions came didn't matter anymore and so with that knowledge I started to speak. I explained to her in as few words as possible that I could not go on for one more day in the amount of pain that I was enduring. I had been suffering all of it in silence for so many years and there was no longer any fight left in me. If there had been any chance for me to regain my health I would have kept trying, but there was nothing more to strive for. My mum sympathised with every aspect of what I had shared. Her reply was that if she had been in my position, she would have given up long before I had. She told me what a strong and courageous person I was to have kept going for all of this time.

As I talked to her in my short form, I wished that I could express myself fully. It was such a significant conversation to be having and yet I could only say the bare minimum and hope that I got my point across. Before I could begin to share my plans with her, my mum said, 'I just need to say one thing.' She then proceeded to summarise a TV show that she had watched only the night before.

The programme documented the true story of a man who had been given a terminal cancer diagnosis. Upon hearing his prognosis, he had become resolved that he would not succumb to his illness. Using the power of his mind alone, he had become healthy again. He had made himself well by taking control of his own body and deciding what was going to happen with his destiny. I found it an enormous coincidence that my mum had watched that particular show the very night before my last day on Earth.

During the past three days I had been replaying 'the girl in the pond' story repeatedly in my head. I couldn't understand what the difference was between her and I or fathom why my trip to the park hadn't worked. I had scrutinised every step of that day, trying to decipher what had gone wrong.

And then there was the other prospect that my body was already well but was simply not recognising the transformation that it had made. The theory was still weighing heavily on my mind. What if I was living that rare possibility and all I needed to do now was to wake my body up? Even if this unlikely proposition *was* true, I was totally clueless about how to make the physical part of me begin to respond appropriately.

I had made the trip to the park by psyching myself into acting like I was able to function properly and yet it had still ended in failure. What else could I try, other than that which I had already done, in order to make either of these scenarios turn into reality? I wished that I could be given a set of instructions that told me exactly what I needed to think and precisely how to act in order to make a miracle happen. Of course, there were none. Nevertheless, when my mum relayed this last astonishing story, I had to pay attention. It was just one too many for me to accept my fate.

All of a sudden the realisation hit me; when I took that trip to the park, I had strived with all my might to somehow make the change happen but had been utterly bewildered as to how to go about it. What if this time I didn't take no for an answer? As this understanding materialised, I felt a rush of determination and a strength of will come over me like I never had before. With that, I declared to myself, 'No more trying, no more wondering how. *JUST DO IT.*'

Since I only had hours to live, it no longer mattered what happened to me, not even if I felt a hundred times worse after what I was about to do. I realised that I had nothing left to lose now except for my fear and with that, it vanished. I reached deep down inside of me, for the last crucial drop of strength, that last ember of fire that had remained burning, even when I had been unaware of it. In that moment, I used it to reignite my very soul. I invoked my raw power and channelled this colossal amount of energy into a one-pointed focus; my transformation. I gathered every last scrap of my energy and determination in order to make the impossible possible.

Instead of *attempting* to make it happen as I had in my previous endeavour, I decided right then and there that I had to believe with all of my heart that it already *had* happened so that there could be no room for uncertainty or hesitation. And so that is exactly what I did, regardless of whether there was any truth to this assertion. In that instant, I made up my mind that my body was well.

I then began my first undertaking; to speak to my mum in a normal manner. Immediately upon commencing this exercise, all of my symptoms began to flare up. The sensations were murderous. But I wouldn't have it. I stated out loud with gusto, 'I need to speak to you.' Initially it felt gruelling to speak. I had to push the words out, shaking as I did so. My symptoms grew more and more adverse. My energy was draining from me and my brain felt like it was going to explode inside my head, but I ignored it all and kept speaking.

After what seemed like aeons but was probably closer to a couple of minutes, I began to feel an almost imperceptible easing of my symptoms. The piercing pain in my head was actually lessening and my stamina began to build ever so slightly. I shared what was happening with my mum; that I was still feeling horrendous, but the intensity of it was improving. Her response was that I should keep talking to her. That suggestion was fine by me.

I had been desperately longing for a chance to express myself for years. There were so many thoughts and emotions trapped inside of me that were yearning to be heard. I began to tell my mum what she meant to me and how much I appreciated all that she had done. I had been wishing that I could say those words to her for such a long time. There was no way to fully convey the level of gratitude that I felt but I could try. I then started to voice my thoughts regarding my life having to end in this manner; how it didn't seem fair to me at all.

Once I began to speak, I could not stop. The flood gates had been opened. I verbalised my feelings about the doctors that had come and gone, the horrific experiences I'd had and the enormity of my symptoms. It was incredible to be able to empty myself of so many of the disturbances that had been buried deep down inside of me for what felt like an eternity. As I continued to talk, my remaining level of breathlessness also began to diminish somewhat.

Not long after I had started to speak, I made the decision to take my industrial strength ear defenders off. I had worn them without interruption for almost three years. When I did so, the new sensation felt completely alien to me. My head felt so much lighter and unrestricted, and it was amazing to be able to move it back and forth on the pillow. I still had my earplugs in but nevertheless, the stark change of hearing noises around me was startling after so many years spent in a world of complete silence.

Even though it was generally quiet, hearing the gentle sounds of the cars going by outside the closed window, my mum's small fidgeting movements, our voices resonating at a louder volume and the seemingly unnoticeable ticks and creaks within the room were all very harsh and overwhelming on both my body and mind. Despite my discomfort I decided that I would never put those ear defenders back on my head again, whether that meant only until the end of the day or for the duration of a future that stretched out into the unknown.

I had no idea what was going to become of me but for the first time in years I wasn't interested. I remained conscious of the fact that this day had only two possible outcomes. The first was that I would be dead by the end of it and all of the pain and suffering would be over. The second was that I would be well. I became resolved to make the last one transpire. I began to recite, with force, both in my head and out loud to myself, 'I am well, my body just isn't aware of it. The symptoms I am feeling are not real because I have already healed.' Every time I felt a doubt or fear creep in, or a symptom begin to increase, I repeated those words.

I contemplated what I wanted to do with what was, potentially, the last day of my life. My first desire was to be clean. Because of how punishing the activity had become for me, I hadn't been able to be washed properly in weeks. The prospect of having a bath was very exciting. My atrophied muscles made it impossible for me to walk and so, upon my request, my mum got me into my wheelchair and wheeled me into the bathroom. It was a struggle but with her help, I made it into the bath, lay down in the shallow water and let her gently wash me.

Tears of joy began rolling down my cheeks as I felt the water running over my skin, the sensation of the sponge on my body and the layers of dirt being washed away. It had been months since I had experienced anything similar. I wished that I could stay in the water forever. However, after only a few minutes, I could sense my body beginning to weaken. The movement, the sensation of touch, the bright light in the room and the loud sounds of the water splashing around had become too much for me. My mum quickly pulled me up and out of the bath so that I could return to bed.

As I crawled from my wheelchair back onto the mattress, I could feel my body collapsing under the strain and all of my familiar and devastating symptoms beginning to serge through me. I reassured myself that all I needed was to rest for a little while in order to give myself a breather after this monumental activity. Since nothing was wrong with me now, my energy levels would pick up again shortly after. Once my body had recovered, I would tackle a new feat.

After about two minutes of lying in bed with the door wide open, listening to the novel sounds of the clean-up process coming from the bathroom I thought, 'These could be the last moments of my life, the last hours in which I have an awareness of the world. I'm not going to waste them.' I repeated my mantras, ignored my body, called my mum into the room and got out of bed.

With assistance I went into the living room where I half sat, half lay on the sofa. I could not believe how wonderful it felt just to be in another room again. It had been over six months since I had last left my bedroom. I absorbed my new environment, noticing with wonder all of the objects' shapes and colours and was amazed by how incredibly intricate everything was. I could not stop marvelling at the sheer spaciousness around me. Soon after entering the room, I made up my mind that I would not leave until the end of the day, no matter how I felt. If it was to be my last, I wanted to enjoy it as much as I possibly could.

Less than a minute in, I began to feel all of my unbearable symptoms re-emerging with a vengeance. My head was pounding, my viral malaise intensifying, the list could go on. I felt an immediate desperation to return to my bed. Instead, I asserted out loud that I was well and therefore, the symptoms I was now experiencing did not need to occur. I would not listen to them. Using a firm voice, I told myself that my body was creating the present reaction because it was the only way it knew how to function. I kept repeating this affirmation over to myself and vowed that I would not give in to all these manifestations.

To my astonishment, after a few minutes they gradually began to fade. I was then able to sit on the sofa with my ear defenders off and speak to my mum in complete sentences. What was happening was almost more than I could comprehend. I thought, 'Just go with it. I am going to put my whole heart into this'. For the first time in over a year I allowed myself to feel enthusiasm.

I remained in the living room from around noon until I went to bed at the very early hour of seven o' clock; the same time as my body had given up on each day in the past. Although I realised that relenting to my exhaustion was a continuation of a long-established pattern, I was willing to let this one slide after all of the amazing accomplishments I had already made. The day ended in a very different manner to how I had envisioned it was going to less than ten hours earlier. What an epic breakthrough I had made.

My achievements had been far from easy. During the hours that I had spent in the living room, I was having to constantly repeat my mantras and fight to resist the overwhelming urge to return to my bedroom and lay back down in the silence. My excruciating symptoms flared up time and time again. In answer to their intrusion, I would relentlessly inform them that they had no business in my life anymore and I was not going to listen to them. After carrying out this action, they would surprisingly back down. Every moment was a mammoth effort.

What I was now attempting was such a giant undertaking. All the while, I was still seriously incapacitated. Even though these phenomenal changes were taking place, to even sit up and speak remained extremely hard for me. When I used all of my willpower, my symptoms would die down no more than to that which I could cope with, never completely disappearing. But *boy,* was that a transformation. Since the beginning of my illness, I had been forced to listen to my body and the copious demands it had put on me. The tables were now, at long last, beginning to turn.

As I lay down in my bed that night, I considered what I was going to have to face when I woke up the next morning. My body could be destroyed from everything I had put it through, or in the same condition as when I went to sleep, or even stronger. I simply had no clue. I was sailing in uncharted waters. My previous plan was still in place to execute if necessary, I was going to have to play that by ear. Nevertheless, I had survived another day and I didn't see why I couldn't manage the next one. That night I went to sleep with hope in my heart for the first time in over a year.

CHAPTER 11

A SENSE OF PURE CONVICTION

When I woke up the next morning, my first panicked thoughts were, 'How do I feel?' Many other fears immediately began to run through my mind. Would I be a thousand times worse than I could have ever imagined possible? Was I going to be able to repeat yesterday's proceedings? Would I try and fail? What if I was unable to find the same level of self-belief to keep the momentum going? My biggest fear was that I had found exactly the right formula for success and if I didn't duplicate this sequence of events, I would be back to square one. I frantically attempted to remember what I had done in order to make the day before possible.

And then I made up my mind to let all of my doubts go and just *make it* happen again. I realised that I didn't need a set of specific instructions or to copy precisely what had occurred during the preceding day. All I needed to hold onto was the decision that I had already healed and all of the viruses and Lyme disease that had been attacking me for so many years had been eradicated from my system. In telling myself this, I was taking away any choice in the matter. If what I was saying was true or not was completely irrelevant. The only role that was required of me was to remind my body of that 'fact' and allow myself to recommence functioning as a healthy human being. With that, I began my day.

Using my mum as support, I struggled out of bed and with difficulty made it into the living room. My breakfast was prepared in front of me for the first time in over three and a half years. Sitting upright on the sofa felt like a dream come true. I didn't enter my bedroom again until the end of the day. I left my headphones off, spoke as much as I desired and listened to my mum talk for as much time as I could bear. I had made the impossible possible yet again.

Even though I was making monumental strides in the right direction, it was still necessary for me to take time to recover quite often throughout the day, although I made sure to remain in the living room while I rested. The purpose of these breaks was to alleviate the psychological distress I was enduring as much as it was to ease my somatic symptoms. I had been laying completely still, in silence, on my own, around-the-clock for so many years now. Being thrown into an environment that was filled with sensations and surroundings I was completely unaccustomed to, was a system overload.

Every aspect of that day was overwhelming. The bombardment on my senses felt like a physical attack. I wanted to run and hide from the world. Simple noises that went on within the house such as the fridge running, the wind outside of the closed windows and the clock ticking were all incredibly difficult to handle. I couldn't tolerate any ordinarily indistinct day-to-day sounds such as my mum getting a plate out of the cupboard or running a tap for instance. The room had to remain very quiet. Not only would my symptoms flare up upon hearing these commonplace noises but I also couldn't cope with them mentally. I realised that I was going to have to go through an extremely slow process of reintegrating myself back into the world again.

Day two of my recovery followed on similarly to day one; with me quietly sitting in the living room. This act alone felt exhilarating. My mum and I spoke as much as we could about the changes that were taking place and what a miracle it all was. After expressing my feelings to her about how demanding it was to simply be in the room, she let me know that she would be there for me every step of the way. We would move at precisely the speed I felt comfortable with. I also voiced how anxious I was feeling about implementing the pursuit correctly. I was panic stricken that if I doubted myself for one second, I would lose all of the progress I had already made. Her response was: 'Carly, let go of the fear, because you are the strongest person I have ever met and I know without a doubt that you can do it.' Her confidence in me was invaluable in this unprecedented circumstance.

As with the day before, I still felt considerably ill. Nevertheless, the simple acts of sitting up and participating in light conversation were enough for me to become full of hope. I was going to stay alive and I was going to be well again. I no longer needed to depend on anyone else to accomplish this. All that was required was my own strength, determination, and belief and, of course, my mum's never-ending dedication and support.

I was reluctant to leave the house for the entire first week as the idea was just too formidable. Finally, one morning, curiosity got the better of me. Although I had lived in the same building for over two years, I had never seen the hallway, the lift, the foyer or outside of the property. When I ventured out for the first time, I was able to visually experience the route that I had taken to the clinic twice daily for such a long period. Nothing looked as it had in my mind's eye. Observing the dissimilarity between the two worlds; that of my creation and that of which was tangible, felt very peculiar but, at the same time, very fascinating.

I had imagined that it would feel heavenly to be outside in the fresh air but sadly, after only a short time in my wheelchair, the sound of the vehicles whizzing past the small path that we were travelling on became terrifying. Every time a car drove by I was convinced that it was going to swerve and hit us. The noise was so loud and powerful that I couldn't bear it and I had to be rushed home after only five minutes. On the way back to our flat I burst into tears from the considerable shock that the low level of stimulation had given me.

My first outing felt comparable to how a seasoned prisoner reacts upon being let out of jail. It could be easy to presume that, after all that time, they would be desperately yearning to leave. But after spending years knowing nothing but the confines of their own cell, often, all the ex-convict wants is to find a way to get back inside. I could empathise very well with that notion when I first came out of my cocoon. I had been trapped within a silent enclosed space for far too long. The outside world was nothing but a distant memory to me now. I waited an entire week before leaving the flat again. On this occasion we were prepared. My mum drove us to a park where I was able to sit still in a quiet spot and absorb my surroundings slowly.

For a few weeks I didn't come to any conclusions about what was happening. I merely took one day at a time. I didn't even tell anyone for the initial week as I was too afraid that the changes wouldn't last. Once I got the confidence, the first person I phoned was my father. When he answered the call and heard a croaky 'Dad', his first reaction was that of panic. He immediately responded with: 'What's wrong? What's happened?'

As I filled him in on everything that had been taking place within the last seven days he was astounded. He could not believe that it was actually me that he was speaking to. It was such a dramatic change to try and wrap his head around. Before the phone call he had been coming to terms with the fact that he might never be able to speak to me again or worse; I might not be alive for much longer. Now here I was, having a full conversation with him, with a level of strength in my voice that he hadn't heard in years. I can remember him saying to me, 'You sound like Carly again'.

I couldn't believe the changes that were transpiring. It took me some time to become certain of the fact that I was able to leave my bed each morning. During the day, my body would announce its dissent to me over and over again in its undying efforts to have me rest. For years I had to heed what it had been telling me but that was now no longer the case. That didn't mean that my mind was able to adjust to this remarkable change overnight. I had taken a very long time to learn to be appropriately attentive to my symptoms. Now I was asking myself to undo all of those years of adherence in the blink of an eye.

In every single instance that I had tried to push through my boundaries in the past, the attempt had ended in incredible disappointment. And when my baseline dropped it could take months for me to recover, all because I had disregarded the messages that my body was sending me. With the terror of severe consequences looming over me for years on end, the old reaction had become ingrained in my psyche; I had learned to fear my body. Each time I now gently pushed myself beyond my limits my mind would automatically respond with, 'What are you doing? The ramifications are going to be horrendous.' I would then remind myself, 'No, this is a new day. I no longer need to listen to my physical symptoms.' No matter how insufferable they were, I would not allow them to take charge.

From the outside it could easily be assumed that if put in my shoes you would have felt euphoric over what was occurring and equally as excited about the possibility of what could happen in the future. But that wasn't how it felt for me at all. The fear that my body could slip back to its bedridden state at any moment was too great and the struggle upon my body too demanding for me to perceive anything but a strong sense of burden. My days were consumed with the battle I was conducting within myself. I had to be brave enough to face my symptoms head on and remain emphatic that they would not get the better of me.

Even though I was now able to influence the intensity of my post-exertional malaise, it had not reduced at all in its frequency. After all that I had suffered, both physically and mentally, having to keep engaging in this unending fight felt exhausting. I couldn't comprehend why my body was aggressively striving to stifle my every attempt to be well. Why wasn't it on my side?

The only weapon that I had with me was the power of my mind.

Throughout the passing days, I constantly faced all of the various demanding symptoms that I had grown so accustomed to. Each time they appeared or grew to an intolerable level, I invoked my mantras and talked myself through them. They would then subside for a while before making a reappearance. It was always difficult to find the right words in order to convince them to calm back down. There was no easy way to do it. I couldn't simply tell them to piss off. There was so much more consideration that went into it. The key was that I remained resolute and unwavering in my convictions. My resolve waxed and waned depending on how strongly I believed that I could make miracles happen, because in effect, that was exactly what I was doing.

I often became petrified that if I did or thought the wrong thing, I would return to bed forever. When I experienced these high levels of anxiety, my symptoms would then increase. From this, I would work myself into an unhealthy cycle of thinking, becoming overwrought because of not being able to redirect my thoughts. In effect, I would panic about panicking. Some of my days were very difficult indeed. But then there were others in which I would feel strong and tell myself that I could do it, I could fight it, my body *would* come around and listen to me in the end and I would persevere until it did.

It was four weeks into my recovery process before I felt any real clarity about what I was doing. This all began when I went to the park in my wheelchair to enjoy some fresh air. On that day I had mistakenly remained there for too long. By the time I arrived home I was in an awful state and had to remain indoors for two days. When my body didn't respond to the rest, I made the decision to go out again, believing that ignoring my post-exertional symptoms would surely put an end to them. Instead of this happening, my energy levels plummeted. For the first time since leaving my bed I had to go back to it. I felt confused by the reaction but surmised that my body hadn't been ready for all that had taken place within the last several days. I reasoned that, as I had pushed myself beyond my limits, I needed to lay down and recuperate for a few hours and then I would be fine.

A few hours turned into a day which turned into three. In the end I was so drained that I became partially immobilised. I was horrified about what was occurring; instead of recovering, I was becoming worse by the day. What was my body doing? Why wasn't it restoring itself with all the rest that it was receiving? I felt completely bewildered for eight whole days before it finally dawned on me; I was giving in to my symptoms. I woke up one morning and thought, 'I AM NOT SPENDING ONE MORE MINUTE IN THIS BED.' I got up and never returned.

That point marked a permanent transition for me. I went from feeling unclear about what was happening, not knowing if what I was doing was the solution, to recognising that I could *make it* the solution. I resolved that I would never listen to my symptoms again. Although I had made that decision, I was nevertheless treading through undiscovered territory. I was completely alone in my endeavours as I had been given no proof that all of my infections were gone. It fell entirely on my shoulders to generate a sense of pure conviction every single day.

Each time I saw an improvement, it would give me the encouragement and inspiration that I needed in order to keep moving forward. Upon witnessing the change, I would become extremely pleased with my progress and filled with optimism about the future. One aspect of my health that I was able to influence remarkably quickly was that of my digestion.

Shortly after leaving my bed I began to focus my efforts on this problem. When I began, I could only tolerate about 15 different varieties of food and had to eat large quantities in order to keep myself from feeling faint. I was sick and tired of ingesting food that I didn't even want. I started to eat a diet that consisted of what I liked, when I liked it, whilst telling my body in no uncertain terms that it would be able to cope with this now. Five days after commencing these new eating habits my intolerances had lessened by approximately 75% and the extreme wooziness had been completely eradicated.

Some changes were fast, others materialised more slowly. My baseline was increasing over time, but this progression was happening so incrementally that it was difficult for me to notice the minute changes that were taking place. Every so often, I would experience moments where I could gauge how far I had come. For a while afterwards my confidence would be restored that I was on the right path.

When I looked back a month or two into the past, I was able to see the evidence a little clearer and think, 'This time last month I wouldn't have been able to complete that task' or 'I wouldn't have felt that well'. My best indicator was when I revisited places or repeated specific activities that I hadn't carried out in a while. These moments gave me a direct comparison to how I had felt during the last time I had been in the same situation.

There was one location in which this occurrence took place on multiple occasions. About 20 miles away from us there was a beautiful park that had a lake in the middle and a path that wrapped all the way around it. Since it was a fair distance from the house, my mum and I wouldn't go very often but every now and again we would make the special effort to get there.

The first time we went there was only a few weeks after I had my miracle day. My mum pushed me almost half of the way around the lake in my wheelchair before I had to be rushed back to the car out of sheer exhaustion. This was the event that had resulted in the short timespan I had gone back to bed. During our second outing to that particular park a couple of months later, I walked half the way around the lake with my mum pushing the wheelchair beside me. It then became necessary for me to sit down the rest of the way. Regardless of this, I felt incredibly proud of my achievement. By the third time I returned, I was able to slowly walk the entire way around the lake on my own. We kept the wheelchair nearby in case I couldn't manage but the need never arose.

During the final outing to the park, I was able to stride around the lake with confidence. I no longer had any fear regarding my ability. I could talk and enjoy the view while I walked rather than having to focus all of my efforts on reaching the goal as had happened during each of the previous visits. I fed the ducks and even spoke to a passer-by for a couple of minutes. We then carried on to have a drink in a cafe afterwards. The transformation that took place in my body over time was made very clear to me during our periodic visits to that park. These were the days that I relished.

In order for this progression to be possible, I had to concentrate on rebuilding all of my muscles. When I first got out of bed my legs were spindly poles. I couldn't walk, both because of the pronounced muscle wastage and my knees not being used to the added pressure. At the beginning, my wheelchair was a necessity at all times. But I quickly started to walk as much as I could, with my mum pushing it alongside of me. In this way, whenever my muscles gave out or my energy depleted, I was able to retreat to the chair. As was to be expected, I also became out of breath very easily after participating in minimal activity. When walking at an average pace or attempting any other gentle movement for longer than a few minutes my heart would race as though it was running a marathon. This muscle also needed time to slowly build upon its strength.

All I wanted was to be completely removed from any thoughts regarding my health, even the healing part of the process. I wished that it could all be over and I could begin a completely new life. Something that helped me in shedding my old existence was when I parted with each piece of medical equipment that I owned. As my body became stronger, I had no need for these items any longer. This gradual clear-out felt very cleansing.

My wheelchair was the most significant remnant to dispose of. During the innumerable hours I had been given to ponder from my bed, I had conjured up countless scenarios of how I would destroy the metal contraption; by setting it on fire, throwing it over our flat's balcony, taking a hammer to it or a combination of all of these things in various orders. In the end I opted for the much simpler solution of giving it to another person in need. I did feel sadness for their particular situation, but I couldn't contain my elation as I handed the wheelchair over and watched it being driven away in the back of another person's car.

When I am now out in public and see someone being wheeled around my heart goes out to them. I can remember the immense sense of powerlessness that came from the lack of control that I had over the direction in which I was heading. Using a wheelchair still has such a stigma attached to it. Because of this, whenever I sat in it I would feel a level of shame, as though my need for one was an indication to others that I was an invalid. I now wish that I could run up to those strangers and say, 'I was once in your shoes and look, anything is possible!' In doing this, I want to give them hope but realise that my gesture could unintentionally provoke the opposite response and so I refrain.

Every time I gave away a piece of my medical equipment it felt like I was moving one inch closer to regaining my health and becoming someone no longer consumed by illness. Even the smaller sized medical items became a pleasure to dispose of. These included packs of tape that had been applied to my hips to help with the aching, arm bands that had eased the intense pain in my elbows and the lap table that I had eaten my food off for years on end. Another symbolic moment for me was when I discarded my CPAP mask. I took a hammer to that one. During the dismantling, I was still unable to look at it without feeling sick. As I smashed the torture device into small pieces, I was moved by both feelings of anger and also triumph for causing its destruction.

The first time I went to see a doctor again, I assumed that they would congratulate me, marvel at my story, give me a physical examination, possibly a handful of blood tests and ask if there was any help that I needed during the next steps of my journey. Disappointingly, I was offered none of the assistance that I had anticipated. At that time, I was still unable to walk more than a few steps on my own and had arrived in a wheelchair. I was contending with many severe symptoms including debilitating exhaustion and general malaise. I had made the appointment as I was feeling extremely depressed and anxious over my circumstances. I needed some support and wasn't sure what I should do.

When I gave the doctor a brief synopsis of recent events, the only actions she took was to suggest that I take an antidepressant and ask me the name of the immunotherapy supplement that I was using. She didn't offer any other form of assistance, not even physical therapy to help with my mobility. Nor did she share any words of encouragement or happiness for my marked development.

I can surmise that the lack of support that I received on that day was at least, in part, due to the fact that the doctor had become aware of the chronic fatigue syndrome diagnosis on my chart; she made sure to comment on it at the beginning of the session. I have no idea why I had still expected to receive any compassion or initiative from the medical profession after all of the appalling experiences I had sustained in the years gone by. In that appointment it became clear that there was no point for me to return unless it was absolutely necessary.

A few months after I got out of bed, my hair began to fall out again quite suddenly. I had no idea why this was reoccurring. By that time, it had been over a year since the hair loss had first taken place and I was now eating a healthy diet. I waited for a couple of months, hoping that it would resolve on its own before finally succumbing to the fact that I needed to make another doctor's appointment. When I was given a blood test, the results came back showing that I had low iron levels.

Less than a week after beginning to take the much needed supplements my hair loss, along with my energy levels, strength, stamina and anxiety all started to improve. It was wonderful to see the grey, drained look leaving my face and the colour returning. My mum would make sure to comment whenever she noticed a positive change, saying things like, 'Your eyes look a little brighter today' or

'Your skin looks rosier'. I also began to feel more lively and energetic into the evening hours whereas previously I had been languishing by about five in the afternoon. It was a very gradual change just like everything else, but it was happening.

Several months into my venture, I realised that I had to stop taking Goleic. By carrying on with the treatment, I was going against everything I was telling myself. All of the time that I was continuing to inject the immune-enhancing protein into my body I was sending my subconscious mind mixed messages; promising one thing and then acting in exactly the opposite manner. If I really believed that the power was in my hands, I would have no problem letting go of my only form of security.

I toyed around with the idea for about a month. I had no confidence in making decisions at that time, even seemingly trivial ones, and so I was very anxious about whether this monumental change was the right move to make. Nevertheless, I felt in my heart that I had to do it. I had to prove to myself that I held full conviction in the words I was using in my mantras every day. This action would determine, once and for all, whether I was still able to be controlled by any of the pathogens that had been thriving inside of my body. In the back of my mind, there had always been a level of doubt over if it was really possible for me to be the sole influence over my recovery or if it was, in fact, the injections that were keeping me from becoming devastatingly ill again.

Every one of my friends and family shared the same opinion: I *must* stay on the supplement at all costs. Whenever I spoke to anyone about it, they would tell me what a bad idea it was to make this decision while I was still feeling so unwell. They would say 'There is no hurry, no need to jump so fast. The Goleic is supporting you, even if you no longer need it. It is, at the very least, strengthening your immune system which can only be beneficial after all that your body has been through. It is not hurting you in any way so why would you choose to stop taking it now?'

All of the comments were made out of love for me but also fear of what the consequences would be. Each time I spoke with someone, I would end up doubting my judgement and come to the conclusion that I must listen to them and wait. It was the sensible thing to do after all. The trouble was that, despite what everyone else was telling me, my heart kept calling and I knew that the action had to be taken before I could fully commit to my endeavours. In my mind, it was more crucial to my recovery for me to fully endorse what I had been telling myself than to be given the extra boost to my immune system. By continuing, every four days, to inject a supplement that's sole purpose was to kill the offending pathogens, I was directly communicating to my body that it could not survive on its own.

In the end, I made the difficult decision to begin the lengthy process of weaning myself off of the immune-boosting supplement. I came down .01ml every time I injected myself which gave me over three months to get used to the idea. About 95% of me was convinced that I no longer had a need for any form of treatment. However, the other 5% was deathly afraid of what would happen. Even so, I followed through with my plan to the end. Although my road to recovery was far from over, never once during the gradual decline did I experience an increase in my symptoms. This was an invaluable experience as it proved to me that the potential to be well was truly within my power. Even more significantly, it taught me the importance of always listening to what was in my own heart.

CHAPTER 12

I AM A PERSON, I LIVE
SOMEWHERE

I felt eternally grateful for being given a second chance at life. Yet the level of inner turmoil that I was now experiencing was almost comparable in intensity to the last few years of my illness. I'd lived inside that one room for so long that the harsh reality of life was too much for me to adjust to so quickly. If my healing had been gradual, as it is in most cases, my assimilation would have been able to be gentle. But there had been such an immediate change. In the span of a few hours I had gone from being almost catatonic to having to try to cope with the world like a fully functioning adult again.

Even though most of the differences were to be substantial improvements from my old life, they were so foreign to me that I found them very difficult to comprehend and absorb all at once. I had to adapt to normal, everyday situations very slowly. From the confines of my bed I had visualised that if I ever began to heal, the process would be an extraordinarily exciting one. I had assumed that the joy would instantaneously flood back into my soul without me having to try at all and I would naturally become the happy, confident person that I used to be. In my mind, this development would transpire for no other reason than because my health was being restored. Disappointingly, reality was not panning out like I had imagined it to. I had never realised just how distressing these next steps would be. I was having to accept that it would take time to readjust and to begin to function again. Time was the only thing I had.

For the first couple of months I felt as though I was living in a dream all of the time. It was such a surreal feeling. I would walk around and talk and do all the usual things a person does but none of it seemed real. Sometimes I would get confused over whether I *was* in a dream. This uncanny misperception only lasted moments but it was very unnerving. During these spells it would appear as though I was looking out at the world from inside of a bubble. I felt completely disconnected from everything including my own self. Sometimes I sensed that I was observing myself instead of being myself. I lived within this dreamlike state for months.

Slowly, as time went by, my world became more real, but it was a gradual process. Soon after leaving my bed, I watched an online video of a girl speaking about the aftermath of being bedridden for years. The way she described her experience was almost identical to that of my own. She gave words to the bubble feeling before I had found a way to explain it to anyone, including myself. Viewing that recording helped to understand and normalise my situation a little. After being shut off from life so completely and for such a lengthy period of time it was inevitable for me to feel a strong sense of detachment.

Over the years that I had been ill, sound had always been the sensation that needed to be avoided most drastically as it had been the most difficult for me to cope with. Therefore, it was now the predominant form of stimulation that caused me to become overwhelmed. Since each noise was new to me, it took time to stop reacting adversely to anything more than the silence I had been accustomed to. Every sound felt shocking and jarring, like a bombardment or an assault to my very being. For anyone who is used to hearing average noises, I imagine the feeling to be akin to someone else sneaking up behind you and blowing a fog horn right in your ear.

During the first few months, while being re-exposed, I had to push myself through this discomfort on a constant basis. Even daily household noises were a challenge for me to cope with. It took about a month for my mum to be able to vacuum the carpet in another room. The washing machine was also afforded a break for about the same length of time. Luckily for us cleanliness was not on our top list of priorities during the first several weeks of my re-emergence.

Established concepts, like the fact that there was an entire world outside of the window, now felt remarkable to me. All I had been able to glimpse for years had been no more than a few feet in front of my face. I could not get over how much space there was everywhere, how vast the sky was and how the land kept going for as far as the eye could see. It took some time to get used to the expansiveness of it all. Whenever I went outside I would think about the fact that, if I had the desire to, I could go as far as I wished in any direction. It felt so incredibly freeing.

The first time we went out for a short drive I couldn't believe how much was taking place on the streets we drove through. There was so much to look at; houses, cars, dogs, children, the list could go on and on. I was floored by how many people there were and the fact that they were all carrying out so many different activities. I realised that each car we passed contained a different person who held their own unique life story. My tragedy was all I had focused on for so long. To be given back this broadened sense of awareness was very meaningful for me. While wasting away in my bed I had lost all sense of being human. Seeing the town that I lived in was one aspect that helped me to begin to remember that I *was* a person; I lived somewhere.

Believe it or not, I even had to adjust to speaking again. At first, I struggled to use more than a small variety of words. I was unaccustomed to hearing speech and so had lost so much of my vocabulary. I imagine this unusual experience to be similar to when a person loses proficiency in their native language after living in a different country for a long period of time. In my case, I had not used my first and only language in years.

I found that my mind had become very slow in its response time. So much so that I wondered if I had suffered brain damage. I had no idea how much of my incapacity could be improved upon by exercising this organ and how much of it was going to be permanent. I had to ask others to speak slowly and was unable to handle focusing on more than one person during a conversation. My short-term memory had also been affected. Sometimes I couldn't remember what I had just done or said only minutes beforehand. I realised that all I could do was try and accept where I was for the time being and remain hopeful that one day matters would improve. Getting myself into this positive mindset was often easier said than done.

Being in the company of others was one of the most challenging factors to readjust to. It seemed like an eternity since I had seen another person's face or heard another voice (other than the occasional word from my mum), let alone tried to participate in any form of communication. Whenever I came face to face with someone I immediately felt out of my depths. I didn't dare to look in their eyes as the intensity of the connection was much too jarring. The noise level that was created when a group of people spoke with each other was incredibly daunting. I had to contend with this at the same time as my brain attempted to focus on the different things being said while simultaneously trying to think of something to respond with. My mind hadn't had to deal with anything that hectic or complex for years.

It took me quite a while to become comfortable within a crowded place. Although I didn't have to speak to those people, the situation was still extremely frightening for me. At the beginning, I couldn't even go into shops as they were too loud and overwhelming. To tackle this, I began to visit only the small, quiet ones first. Then, once I felt ready, I started to purposely ask simple questions to the shop owners. I felt very anxious over each exercise but knew it was all part of the process of becoming a person again. As with all other aspects of my rehabilitation, I had to take one baby step at a time.

I also felt uneasy with the people who I had been closest to. It took about a month after my 'miracle day' for me to begin to have proper conversations with my father and two friends on the phone again. As bizarre as it may seem, it was another big step for me. I found it difficult to know what to say to them or how to express myself correctly but slowly, I began to relax and feel more comfortable.

I was amazed that my loved ones were able to perceive my situation as well as they did. It was obvious to me that they had each taken the time to truly consider what those years must have been like and because of this effort, they were now able to express deep empathy with my struggle. The love and kindness that they showed during our talks enabled me to learn how to communicate adequately again. I felt such sincere appreciation for having them in my life.

During our talks, I noticed that my father's insight into what I had been through had improved substantially. In the past he had always been supportive but had found it difficult to relate to my experiences and emotions with any depth of feeling. Once I began to speak to him again he was incredibly receptive. He listened attentively and always seemed to know exactly what to say to validate my past ordeals. He went out of his way to provide anything I needed in order to further my healing. I felt extremely grateful for his care.

My mum had not changed an ounce. She remained my anchor throughout the entire storm that was still bellowing within me. I knew without a doubt that she would always be there, no matter what and I felt incredibly lucky to have her standing beside me. My mum never ceased to amaze me with the level of sensitivity that she showed. She had no first-hand experience and yet, just as with all the past years of my illness, was able to deeply understand every emotion that I now felt. Without her I would have been lost.

Every time I spoke with my friends and family they expressed their awe over how quickly my body was gaining strength and the way in which I was acclimatising back into the world. No matter how positively they felt, I remained consumed with worry, thinking that I should have been able to progress faster than I was, not only physically but mentally too. I was constantly feeling discouraged and angry over the fact that I couldn't heal quicker or function like a normal person.

In response, my loved ones would tell me that I shouldn't expect any more than exactly what was unfolding. For a few days after speaking with them, our conversation would instil a sense of patience within me and a realisation of how lucky I was to be at that exact point along my path. Sadly, soon afterwards, I would become frustrated with myself again. I carried the deep-seated fear around with me at all times that this battle would be never ending. I had spent so many years feeling immobilised. Even though things were actually improving, I was panic-stricken at every stage that they would become static again.

When I first caught sight of my own image again after three and a half years, it felt as though I was looking into the eyes of someone else. Nothing resembled the person I remembered being. I had not seen a mirror even once in all that time and so it came as a huge shock to view my appearance's seemingly instantaneous ageing. I hadn't witnessed my body slowly deteriorating from the lack of nutrients and the diseases that had been raging within me. Because of this I now appeared to be twenty years older rather than three.

My hair was a mess; it had been cut short and jaggedly and was very thin. Before becoming bedridden, it had been blonde in colour but because of being indoors for so long it had since turned a mousy brown. In the last months I had gained about three and a half stone in my attempts to avoid the feelings of extreme wooziness. The extra weight now made me almost unrecognisable. My skin was covered in spots and was lacking any sort of healthy glow. Instead it looked sallow, drawn, and grey. Even my eyes were faded and weak as a result of all of the suffering that I had endured. From that point onwards, every time I looked in the mirror I would cry. I covered them at first so that I wouldn't have to be reminded of what I had become.

I spent every waking minute feeling lost and inhuman and confused about who I was. Because of this, making the simplest of decisions was impossible. But as the weeks passed, I slowly became involved in commonplace activities. These proved effective in helping me regain some trust in myself and the choices I made. One of them that I remember in particular was shopping to buy new clothes. Let's face it, what circumstance wouldn't that help!

All I had worn during the first years of my illness was old tracksuit bottoms and comfortable tops. In the final years this had been reduced to only nightshirts. There were clothes stored away in boxes from eight years previous, but I had changed quite substantially since then. These items belonged to the old me, the girl from the past. At first, I found it difficult to discern what I liked and disliked. I would look at each item of clothing and think, 'Is *this* me? What *is* me?' As I tried on piece after piece, I slowly began to discover my preferences.

Through self-expression and everyday experiences, a person creates an image of who they are. I had been fundamentally starved of both of these ordinary occurrences for far too long. I had to relearn what specifically made me feel good. Buying new clothes sounds like a trivial distraction, but activities of this nature were very grounding for me. They gave me a sense of identity when I felt that I had none, which helped to ease the shakiness a little bit.

It was all of the simple things that were bringing me back, little by little, to who I was, like being able to shave my legs again after so many years. Instead of this hairy being that I had come to know, I now felt soft and feminine. Re-piercing my ears and nose was another step that brought me closer to being me again, like one more piece of the puzzle was being put into place.

For so long now, the illness had been the only thing to define who I was. It had consumed me and, in the end, had become my whole identity. All of these small shifts were slowly taking me away from it and guiding me towards who I was becoming; a person. I was bringing myself back from the dead; a little of the old mixed in with a little of the new.

A few weeks into my recovery, I rushed head first into losing the weight that I had gained during my period of insatiable 'hunger'. Before this, my figure had always leaned towards the slender side. The additional weight that I now carried was a considerable amount for my height. The fact that my image was so unfamiliar was not helping matters when I already felt so lost. I also didn't feel healthy. It took so much more energy to carry out physical activities that were already taxing on my body in the weakened state that I was still in.

In order to shed the excess kilos, I immediately cut down on the large amount of food that I had grown accustomed to eating while also making sure to maintain a healthy diet. My body's first reaction was to revolt. But as the familiar wooziness kicked in, I fought back; with mantras. I told those symptoms to pipe down, just as I had with all of the others. I would eat normally and that was that. Once I had the situation under control, it took me approximately six months to reach my old weight. I realised that these actions might have been demanding on my body. However, the tremendous amount of benefit that I received from being able to recognise a part of myself as I had always known it was indispensable to me.

Gradually, I took on small tasks to overcome, though they had to remain simple or I would become overwhelmed very quickly. At the beginning, it was as basic as getting food out of the fridge in preparation for the dinner that my mum would cook. This was another avenue I used to figure out how to function on a basic level and to operate like a human being again.

As the months went by, I witnessed my progression evolving naturally. I kept trying new things every day and didn't give in to the incessant fear that lived inside of me. However, It was important to focus on keeping a balance between pushing too little and pushing too much. I found this part to be very trying indeed as I had the tendency to expect too much of myself.

Although I was making some incremental steps to assist in my rejuvenation, I was having trouble coming to terms with the fact that I had lost nearly a decade of my life to this insufferable disease. Since I was 24 years old, discounting having to fight for my health and all of the heartache that came with it, my experiences had been few. Within these years, many of my friends and similarly aged family members had gotten married, had children, moved, bought their first homes, begun to work and eventually progressed within their chosen occupations. They had participated in events like concerts, birthday parties and holidays while I had been sitting on the sofa or laying in my bed.

In many ways I still felt like I was in my early twenties even though I had been 'resurrected' at the age of 32. This large age gap brought my attention to all of the years that had been stolen from me. I felt such resentment towards my illness as well as the doctors for making no effort to find my real diagnosis sooner. There was so much anger inside of me for all of the years that had been taken away. They were now over and there was no way for me to get them back.

However, there were *some* gifts to come out of this experience. Through the loss, I gained an innumerable amount of positive reintroductions to the world. I had so many second 'first' experiences, that I began to call myself a born-again virgin. I was constantly using the phrase, 'This is my first time' when I really meant that it had been a long time since I had felt a certain source of pleasure. There were so many wonderful moments, like when I listened to my 'first' music album; *Disintegration* by The Cure. Upon playing the opening song, memories of a past life immediately flooded back to me. I cried as I was opened up to emotions that had long since been forgotten.

Another exceptional experience was when I laughed wholeheartedly for the first time. It had been so long since I had been given a reason or had the necessary physical capabilities to engage in this thoroughly enjoyable but also highly strenuous activity. The action of releasing joy from my heart was powerful beyond measure. Not all of my pleasurable 'firsts' were main events. Things like eating pizza and ice cream, going to the cinema and walking around a park on my own were equally as wonderful in their own ways.

I had been removed from society for so long that upon my return it felt as though I was an alien landing on another planet. I could also compare the sensation to how it would feel after being put into a time machine and sent hurtling into the future. There were current affairs to catch up on and differences in attitudes, fashions and technology. Some elements had changed so much that I could hardly recognise them. Others had stayed the same but were beyond my recall anyway. I was completely out of touch.

The average person may not even notice fashion trends evolving slowly over time. My experience was different as I was thrown from one fad directly into another. People were also using new slang words to express themselves. It took me a while not to want to laugh whenever I heard the phrases being repeated. When I was first reintroduced to music, I could identify just how prolifically musicians depend upon each other to create their work. All forms of art grow and morph as the world does, but it was strange for me to witness this slow progression accelerated. I have always been aware of the tendency for people to emulate one another but the novelty of my circumstances brought it home to me even more.

I was pleasantly surprised when I learned that the United States had legalised same-sex marriage. I had always hoped that, eventually, the day would come but was delighted to find out that it had already occurred. I also noticed a corresponding overall shift in the attitudes of the general public regarding sexual orientation, especially within the younger generation. It was a refreshing transformation and, in my personal opinion, one of the greatest that I witnessed.

The most obvious and somewhat disturbing change that I had to adjust to was the fact that everybody now played out their lives on their smartphones. Before I became encapsulated within my room, a mobile phone was a mobile phone. They had looked nothing like they did now. When I properly ventured out of the house for the first time, I was shocked to see that hardly anybody was actually relating in the real world. They were instead, all glued to their screens, listening to music and speaking into what appeared to be thin air. I was having to constantly remind myself that many of the people I walked by on the street were not actually emotionally unstable but merely conducting a phone conversation using virtually undetectable headphones.

It deeply saddened me that people were rarely participating in their lives first-hand anymore. At enjoyable events, instead of concentrating on what was in front of them, most people were taking photos and videos of it. In the company of others, rather than communicating with those around them, they were busy texting. It was as if everyone had placed an intentional barrier between themselves and the world. After being unwillingly starved of experience and pleasure for so long, I found it tragic that people were frequently making the conscious choice to disconnect from any real sensations.

Some of the changes I considered to be positive, others to be negative, most fell somewhere in between. But each of them made me feel like an outsider. Occasionally, it all became so disconcerting that I felt like I wanted to crawl into a ball, lay back down in my bed and pull the covers over my head. However, I was adamant that I would NEVER EVER do this. It didn't matter how strong the opposing sentiment was, the need to live was more compelling.

What kept me going despite it all, was the recognition that this was the last part of the battle. If I fought for just a little longer, I might actually be able to have my life back again, and I couldn't let that opportunity pass me by. I knew that I had to continue taking one step in front of the other, even though it felt like I was climbing a mountain so high that I would never be able to reach the summit.

Right in the midst of this tumultuous time, I decided to take a trip away on my own. I felt instinctively that it was exactly what I needed in order to be able to rediscover my autonomy and strength. Although my muscles and heart had been growing slightly stronger and my baseline was slowly increasing, my mental health seemed as if it was remaining stagnant. I wanted to be given the chance to gradually adjust to being in the company of others again and yet found that I was never in the position to make that happen. My mum and I didn't know anyone in the town where we lived and although we visited family occasionally, the three-hour round trip was still very tiring for me on top the actual visit. Because of the continuing seclusion, my socialising skills were being given no chance to progress. I felt trapped within my current situation.

There was also the other side of the coin to contend with. On the day that I had gotten out of bed, within a matter of seconds my life had switched from total isolation to being in the presence of another person 24/7. I must confess that, after being completely alone for such an extended period, I did not feel at ease in my mum's company all the time. I *was* very grateful for it but only in little doses. What I really craved was the solitude that I had grown so accustomed to. I needed to be able to build up human contact in small increments. This was another reason why I knew that I had to leave.

This lack of development could also be seen in my dependence levels. My mother and I were enmeshed in the same caregiver and receiver roles that we had known for years. She had become so accustomed to her role as protector and caregiver that she was finding it difficult to adjust to me being a semi-functioning adult. I had to repeatedly remind her that it was now safe for me to begin to take care of myself again. I felt that if I remained at home any longer it would be impossible to ever find my independence. On top of this, I was still living in the flat where all of the trauma had taken place. I was desperate to break out of the web that I had been caught in. I didn't take the decision lightly or think that it would be easy. However, I felt that being thrust into a new environment was essential for me to make any headway. In doing this, it would be imperative that I learned to rely upon myself again, otherwise I would flounder.

Honestly, after all that she had been through, I think my mum was as much in need of the break as I was. She had focused solely on my needs for the last eight years of her life and felt utterly exhausted from the highly demanding role that being a full-time carer entails. Her routine had been so regimented and the worry so great that she had long ago lost her sense of self. Even though I had begun to be less of a cause for her concern as of late, she was finding it difficult to know how to adjust to the changes and what to do with her new found time and energy. Being given some space away from me would provide her with a period of respite; a chance to relearn what it was like to simply 'be' again.

Not one person I knew agreed with my plan. Everyone I spoke to was extremely frightened for me and could not believe that I wanted to go travelling when I was still feeling so ill. The concerns that they voiced included, 'What if you become seriously ill when you are out on your own? This is too fast; you are pushing yourself and your body too hard. After all you have been through you need to take things slowly'. They couldn't fathom why I would make such a rash decision and wished that I would reconsider.

Again, their reaction was born out of love and concern for my welfare. I understood where they were coming from but regardless of this, my resolve did not waver for one second. I held on to my strong sense that this journey was going to help me in so many ways that would be impossible while living in the same house, hemmed in by all of those old familiar patterns and memories. Before I became well, my aunt and uncle had generously given me some money as a gift. Seven months after leaving my bed, I used it to pay for an amazing two-month trip to Bali; a place that happened to be situated on the other side of the world, as far away as I could possibly get from my present circumstances.

At the time of my departure, I was still not out of the woods by a long way. When I did any activity, my body would want to rest and recover. I no longer suffered any lasting repercussions, but the reduced level of post-exertional malaise that remained was always a struggle to contend with. My muscles had become strong enough to cope with everyday levels of light activity, but I couldn't partake in any form of gentle exercise or lengthier walks. Yet for some reason I was convinced that the adventure I was about to embark on was exactly what I needed in order to recover fully.

The immensity of my ambition didn't hit me until after I had entered the airport. The minute my mum left my side I became highly alarmed and thought, 'What am I *doing*? I'm not ready for this. I'm not strong enough. What was I *thinking*? Eight weeks is too long.' I was petrified. I almost had a panic attack in the airport but brought myself back from it by saying, 'JUST DO IT. Whatever happens, it will be an experience. Just get on that aeroplane.' And that was exactly what I did. I walked through the airport to my departure gate and stepped onto the plane.

I embarked upon the long and confusing journey and remained busy talking myself out of a panic attack for almost the entirety of the 18-hour trip. It was the first instance that I had done anything on my own, made any important decisions or felt any sort of independence. As there was a layover, I had to find my next flight on time with hardly anyone speaking English. I wasn't thoroughly confident that I could do it, but I became determined. After so many years without having the responsibility of carrying out daily tasks, the day's proceedings were a giant undertaking for me. Once I finally made it to my destination and had accomplished this first completely autonomous act, I felt a slight rise in my level of self-belief.

In spite of this, my acute feelings of apprehension and panic continued for about a week after I arrived in Bali. I was fearful of every little thing as it was all so new. I had no one by my side to turn to if anything became confusing or complicated or if I simply felt outside of my comfort zone. It was a huge adjustment but such a positive one for me to make. I began to work through my nerves and slowly build up my strength. Every time I achieved something on my own, I would feel slightly more brave. Not to say that the progression followed in a straightforward line. I had many moments of feeling unstable and tremendously vulnerable. These debilitating feelings waxed and waned during the entirety of my trip.

Quite often during those two months I would phone home in a state of hysteria. I felt so incredibly anxious and lonely and didn't know how to cope with the intensity of these feelings. Nothing felt solid or secure ... *ever*. Sometimes I wished that I was home, safe and sound, with my mum looking after me again. But instead, I would push through whatever the current circumstance was that was scaring me and realise that in actuality, I could do anything. Having power over one's own existence is a basic characteristic of being a healthy, functioning adult. It was the first time in nine years that it had been possible for me to feel that way.

Being able to have this experience was, in part, due to the fact that I had been afforded some much-needed space away from my loved ones. Because of their deep level of concern about my welfare, each of them were endeavouring to cocoon me inside the safety of their arms. The knowledge that they were there, no matter what, was indispensable to me. However, what I honestly needed now was to be able to test the waters a little and ask for their help whenever I felt like I couldn't cope on my own.

Although at this time, the urge to reach out happened to be often, it was vital that I be given the chance to rebuild confidence in myself and learn to trust in the virtues of life again. At times it could be terrifying but whenever an incident turned out OK despite my trepidation, it provided me with some assurance that the world would not come crashing down around me.

Some aspects of the trip were draining and overwhelming but others were incredible. One of the highlights was when my closest friend came to visit me from America for ten days. Spending quality time with someone my own age was tremendously uplifting. After living without the merits of friendship for so many years, I had begun to believe that it was impossible for anyone to like me. Being around a trusted friend again helped me to realise that simply being me was enough.

There was one occasion during her stay in which I actually felt happiness and excitement; two emotions that I hadn't experienced in years. We spent the entirety of that day participating in fun activities including visiting hot springs and temples. I began the morning in my normal state of mind, feeling jittery and despondent. However, after a few hours I sensed a sliver of pleasure slowly creeping into my field of consciousness. As the day progressed, the response came on stronger and stronger until eventually, happiness filled my heart and soul.

I couldn't believe how invigorating the feeling was. After so many years spent without joy, I had completely forgotten what it was like. I kept repeating, 'I can't believe how happy I am! It feels so amazing!' I could imagine the frequency at which I was saying those words was quite annoying for my friend and yet I wasn't able to contain myself. Pure delight was spilling out of me. It lasted for a few hours before receding, but for my 'first' encounter it had been ample.

I had chosen Bali specifically as my destination because of its spiritual and calm atmosphere and picturesque landscape. As I had envisaged, the surroundings provided me with the tools that I needed to be able to grow and change. After being starved of beauty for such an incredibly long time, I craved any sort of pleasure to the senses. Whilst in this country, I received copious amounts, in all of its varying forms. Each time I was lucky enough to have another pleasing encounter it felt like I was giving myself a gift, one that had been taken away from me for far too long. There were many special instances that I can recall, including waking up early to watch the sun rising over the ocean, seeing the most beautiful views from on top of a high hill, being fully conscious of all of the colours in the sky during a particularly spectacular sunset and watching tiny leaves sparkling in the sunlight as they floated slowly down to a river's edge from a very high height.

I sensed the sheer pleasure of my vitality returning while swimming in the fresh clear water at the base of a waterfall or following a narrow dirt path through lush rainforest. It was at these times that I could literally feel my muscles and heart coming alive again. My spirit soared when visiting temples where I had time to feel the peace of my surroundings and smell the fragrant incense filled air.

This reaction also occurred whilst becoming acquainted with the exotic flavours of the fresh local food that contained delectable Indonesian spices. As I ate the delicious meals, I remained aware of the wholesome nutrients that my body was receiving; another enormous gift that I was now able to give to myself. Much of my time was spent sitting quietly within my own company, listening to the stillness layered with occasional soothing sounds of nature such as beautiful bird song and the wind moving through the trees. I gained so much pleasure from all of these simplicities.

After I had been in Bali for a few weeks I decided to spend some money on a professional massage. That experience provided me with the first in-depth sensation of touch that I had received in almost a decade. Because of my extreme deprivation, during the entire session it was as though each and every nerve ending was coming alive again with pleasure. Honestly, there was no need for the masseuse to carry out any special techniques. The act of touch alone was enough to make me feel like I was in heaven. Upon their reawakening, all of my senses had been heightened.

I came across various therapeutic modalities along the way such as meditation and yoga, and immersed myself in them. They became instrumental in the facilitation of my healing. For the first month I participated in yoga classes almost every day. As it is such an adaptable form of exercise, I was able to practise at the pace that I was comfortable with and build from there. It was a gentle workout that allowed me to reconnect to and establish a positive relationship with my body again.

All of the walking and yoga that I participated in during these months improved my physical strength substantially. In place of my spindly poles for legs I began to see my calf and thigh muscles re-emerge. Feeling physiologically stronger also affected me psychologically as I no longer identified myself as the weak, unhealthy person that I had once been. What a lovely way to regain my vigour; by engaging in activities that I wholeheartedly enjoyed.

Most of the duration of my trip was spent in solitude. Being afforded this quality time with myself while doing things that I took pleasure in was invaluable. It was essential for me to be able to reflect, relearn how to listen to my own inner voice and begin to build a compassionate awareness of myself again. I received so much from quietly sitting or moving through my surroundings. Having said that, the intermittent talks I had with fellow travellers were also greatly beneficial for my recovery. I found my typical day to be interspersed with small amounts of contact such as sitting amongst a group in meditation or having a small conversation with an individual in a cafe.

Despite having all of these wonderful adventures, I was still so very fearful. I felt wildly anxious, deeply depressed and completely numb almost all of the time. Each day was an enormous challenge for me from beginning to end. I became distressed when having to plan out what I was going to do next, especially when I had to change locations.

Every time I left a place, I got agitated and panicky the day before and during the move. Luckily the anxiety would subside somewhat once I had reached my destination, seen my new surroundings and become settled into where I was to be for the next couple of weeks. Despite this adversity, my confidence began to emerge as I had to adjust to each new and exciting environment that I discovered. It seems to be the case that the most difficult experiences in life are the ones in which we grow from the most.

One day, towards the end of my two-month trip, it dawned on me that I had stopped having to convince my body that the illness was over. It crept up so slowly that I didn't even realise the change until it had already happened. Before leaving for Bali I had been terrified that I would never be well. My focus and drive had remained 100% on the goal at all times. However, it was not through any form of pushing or trying that my full personal transformation had occurred. In the end, I achieved my aspiration by participating in new experiences, feeling pleasure in all of its many forms and giving myself the time to simply be. My travels had provided me with the perfect ingredients to foster my own healing.

Although I still felt low levels of fatigue and weakness, my main symptom of post-exertional malaise had finally retreated into the abyss. After almost exactly nine years of living with this immense weight around my neck; this demanding, exhausting, debilitating burden, I had finally been liberated from its monstrous clutches. Never again did my energy plummet during or after any activity I carried out, be it mental or physical. I had no more cognition issues, headaches or sensitivities to sound, touch or sight. Add that to the already resolved symptoms of breathlessness, PoTS, joint pain and stomach issues and you find one thoroughly delighted individual.

While looking around a shop one day I came across some sky lanterns like the ones my friends and family members had sent up on my birthday, filled with implorations for my healing. I decided to buy one and have my own ceremony. It was the quintessential way for me to be able to give thanks to the universe for granting their wishes and also my own.

I wrote my thank you message on the white paper balloon for all of the many blessings that I had received. That night, I walked out into a secluded field in the darkness, with nothing but the stars to light my way. I lit the lantern and released it into the sky, watching as it floated higher and further into the distance. I stood in the silence and whispered my thanks until the glowing orb had disappeared entirely from my sight.

On the last day, just before returning home, I got a tattoo in order to honour my second chance at life. There were so many aspects of my healing that I wanted to capture within one concept and so I struggled to think of a design that would cover everything. Then I realised that all I needed to have inscribed was the date that my life had changed forever; the date that I had gotten out of bed. I had it placed around my wrist in Balinese script. As soon as it was finished, I felt like it had always been a part of me.

The permanency of that mark helps me to remember all that I have been through. My intention is not to feel pity for myself but instead to always cherish how truly fortunate I now am. Most significantly, I had the tattoo done so that I would remain fully aware of the strength of will that I possessed in order to facilitate my transformational healing with the power of my own mind. The symbolism is a constant reminder that with self-belief and determination, anything is possible.

The lengthy trip provided me with exactly what I had hoped for. It had been a voyage and an adventure, both literally and figuratively. I learned so much during my time there, including how to begin to trust in myself and my decisions and that when I listened to my heart things often turned out the way I wanted them to. In short, I found myself again. After an eight-week hiatus I returned home to the real world. As soon as my mum met me in the airport, she could see that I had changed. The journey was not over yet, I still had so much further to go. Nevertheless, simply learning how to be in my own skin had been a momentous step in the right direction.

CHAPTER 13
THAT MYTHICAL DEMON

The time away had allowed me to see that I could function autonomously on a basic level. I had become a person again and had also experienced some real joy. Most significantly, it was in Bali that my body had stopped fighting for ultimate control. That period of respite had given me time to reflect and grow without the pressures of everyday life encroaching on me. I wish that I could say that it was all flowers and rainbows from that point on but if I want to be truthful, I cannot do that.

My seemingly unending struggle to be well was finally over and yet I could not distinguish this monumental shift for what it was. I still felt moderately drained, tired and weak all of the time and had no idea what was causing these lasting symptoms. I was also experiencing heart palpitations on a regular basis, especially during any form of light exercise including walking. I remained highly anxious, wondering if my body had simply been overburdened for far too long and the ramifications were to be permanent.

Because of all of the years that I had spent worrying over and focusing on my health, I was unable to stop myself from continuing to panic and obsess about it. My mind reran the same disturbing thoughts innumerable times each and every day. Eventually, I reluctantly made a trip to the doctors with my concerns and had blood taken, but other than continuing to have low iron, no other results came back abnormal.

Once I had returned home, I found that the world was much more formidable than I had remembered it to be. My anxiety flooded back in abundance and with it so did my depression. During the eight weeks away, it hadn't been necessary to carry out all of the duties of a fully functioning adult. My daily needs had been met; my room was cleaned, my washing done, my food cooked. My only job had been to focus on myself and what I wanted out of the day.

There were now so many decisions to make and tasks to be completed. Simple responsibilities such as housework, shopping for food and deciding on what I was going to prepare for meals were extremely daunting. All I wanted was to be autonomous but here I was, continuing to depend on my mum to take care of my needs. The only difference from the past was that this time it was for psychological reasons rather than physical.

My mind worried incessantly and there was nothing I could do to stop it. Because of this I was unable to concentrate on the present moment. My anxiety was so elevated that any sort of tiny occurrence would cause me to fall to pieces. I could have no plans for the day but still find myself becoming wound up over simple things like having a shower, emptying the rubbish or remembering to take something out of the freezer for dinner. I was constantly writing down overly detailed lists as otherwise I would panic that I could forget something incredibly important.

I hated the fact that I couldn't manage to function and judged myself harshly on it. I had been given my life back. Therefore, in my mind, I should have been ecstatically happy. I ought to have been over the moon to do anything at all after being basically catatonic. The level of disappointment and humiliation that I felt in myself was enormous. I came to the assumption that others would judge me in the same manner and worried that I was falling short of their expectations.

The life I now led seemed empty to me. I had no friends within visiting distance, no money, no job and no place that I felt was home. Having this blank slate could be viewed as exciting. It could be seen as a chance to create a new world for myself and mould it exactly the way I wanted it to look. But because of the distraught state that I was in, this was terrifying for me. Although I was repeatedly told by my loved ones that all of it would come in time, I found it exceedingly difficult to be patient. I wanted to know what my purpose was and yet I wasn't ready to take the steps to find it, not when I couldn't even put a load of washing on.

About twice a month I would have a phone conversation with my father or one of my friends from America. Other than that, and the ample time that I spent with my mum, I was on my own. My extreme sense of loneliness only led to more depression. I knew that I needed connection but, because of my nerves, I couldn't take the steps that were required to make friends. It was a catch-22.

When I had first arrived home from Bali, I assumed that my confidence would begin to build slowly on its own. As a result, I pictured that I would be able to take on small tasks and adjust to them, one after another, until eventually I was able to function normally again. At that point, I had trusted that time would heal all wounds. It was now becoming obvious to me that this wasn't to be the case.

Over a year had passed since I had gotten out of bed, and I was still in exactly the same place psychologically that I had been in when I returned home from my trip away. Nothing had changed even slightly. I was caught in my own personal nightmare with no means of escape. I had fought so hard for my life. However, now that I had it again the mental torture was so severe that I was not sure that I wanted to live.

I had never, for one moment, conceived that I would feel like this. During the nine years that I had struggled, desperately fighting to get to the place that I now found myself in, all I ever imagined was that if I did actually become healthy again, my life would be perfect in every way. This was miles away from my current circumstance. I finally realised that nothing was going to change until I figured out why this was happening.

Through researching online, I found information about a specific form of anxiety called post-traumatic stress disorder (PTSD). Reading through the extensive list of symptoms, I discovered that many of them corresponded with my own. The condition often manifests after someone has been exposed to a traumatic event. The person afflicted will then experience intense or prolonged psychological distress and/or physiological reactions when facing anything that provokes a memory or a link to the trauma. I had many triggers including being ill, being alone, being in bed or even seeing objects that I had used during the time I was incapacitated.

If anything at all activated thoughts about an aspect of the last few years of my illness I would immediately remove myself from the situation. If that wasn't possible, my breathing would speed up, my heart pound and I would experience feelings of panic, lack of control and something called disassociation. This particular state of being can develop as a coping mechanism to help a person deal with especially high levels of stress.

Whenever the sensation occurred, I felt detached from reality including my surroundings and emotions. It was a strange feeling, a bit like being in a dream or a bubble. As previously mentioned, I had lived in this state of disconnection on a constant basis during the first couple of months after getting out of bed. During these episodes, I lost the ability to concentrate properly on what was happening and felt spacey, nauseous and dizzy. My blood pressure would also drop, making me feel cold, weak, and light-headed.

There were many other symptoms of the disorder that I could relate to, including the fact that I couldn't remember a lot of the events that had taken place during those years. When I tried to bring certain situations to mind, I was met with large, blank spaces in time. Honestly, I was grateful for the emptiness as I had no desire to recall any of it but was also aware that this inability was a bit strange. Everything that had happened was so horrific that it seemed illogical for me not to be able to remember all of the details.

I now had such low self-esteem. This made no sense to me as in the past I had always been such a confident person. I felt like a total failure. Partly because I was unable to stand on my own two feet, but I also sensed it in general; in the views I had about myself, the way I looked, the way I acted and the things I said. I didn't like myself or feel worthy of love. I had no interest in doing the activities that I used to enjoy before I became ill and had lost the ability to feel any positive emotions. It felt as though a thick fog had descended over me, and, try as I may, there was no way of lifting it.

I was completely detached from my surroundings including the people I cared for the most. I couldn't feel love for anyone anymore, including my mum, my dad and my friends. I knew that I should have been feeling a deep affection towards these people who had done nothing but cared for and shown kindness towards me and yet I couldn't. My utter lack of attachment was shocking to me and I feared that I would feel this way for the rest of my life.

This state of numbness towards others was all-encompassing. If anything happened to the people I loved or to the world in general, whether it be good or bad, I simply had no reaction. Even my dog was not exempt from my lack of warmth. When she was finally able to return home, I felt no pleasure from being in her company. It didn't matter how much I craved the intimacy of love and connection; I was unable to feel either of them. I, instead, felt so utterly alone and isolated from the world.

The unnerving anxiety and depression that consumed me now were the only emotional states that I could seem to sense. All of my thoughts and feelings revolved around my own experience. Even though I was ashamed of this, I couldn't seem to change it. I was constantly in a state of anger that got directed towards the only person around me; my mother. The one person that deserved my love, kindness, and patience was now bearing the brunt of my irritability.

I had problems concentrating, difficulty with sleep and would wake up early and abruptly every morning in a heightened state of panic. Although these issues had dramatically improved from the time that I was ill, there was now a psychological reason for them instead of a physical one. I was experiencing hypervigilance, meaning that I remained constantly alert and on edge in order to foresee any perceived danger. Worrying about and trying to control everything was absolutely exhausting. As soon as I lost my nerve, my automatic response was to disassociate. There was no controlling my overreaction and quite often I would spend days on end in this strange foggy state.

It came as such a relief to have been able to read about my condition. Doing this helped me to understand my symptoms and why I was experiencing them. My reactions were actually quite typical for the level of trauma I had endured. This realisation helped to lessen my continuing feelings of guilt, confusion, frustration and shame and to normalise what I was going through. I had a disorder that could be treated but I couldn't do it alone, I needed help.

Once I had realised this, I made an appointment with a therapist who specialised in PTSD. After a thorough assessment, she told me that I had the complex form of the disorder. This occurs when a person experiences a traumatic event over a prolonged period of time. Instead of being exposed to one short lived incident, such as a car crash, mine had been stretched out over many years.

A person with Complex PTSD has other symptoms alongside the standard ones, including a high occurrence of emotional flashbacks. I would constantly relive intense emotions that I had during the trauma, fully believing that they were a justified reaction to my present circumstances. Disassociation is also one of the predominant factors of the specific disorder along with feelings of helplessness, despair and being easily overwhelmed. I was ticking all the boxes.

The bulk of my condition had developed from what I had mentally sustained during the last three years of my illness. Although there were aspects of the situation that had been disturbing years before they had become traumatic, I don't believe that I would have had

PTSD if I had not become bedridden. For example, I had felt disregarded from the beginning, but it wasn't until the last few years that the disrespect had become detrimental to my health, causing me a fear of death or being committed. That was the time when it had produced the real damage.

The deepest and darkest deprivation I had sustained during those three years was the utter lack of power I had felt over my own destiny. During this time, all sense of control had been wrenched away from me and placed into the hands of the medical professionals. These ignorant people had been unwilling to listen to anything that I thought or felt even though they had no clue about what was really happening to me.

This dismissive attitude was compounded by the fact that physically I could do nothing to make myself heard. I had no voice both literally and figuratively. I felt as though I had been attacked and pinned down to the ground by somebody much stronger and heavier than I was. I had been fighting with all of my strength to protect myself but however hard I fought, it was impossible to get back up.

With all of this metaphorical pressure on top of me, I had felt cornered in and full of fear. I had no way of shielding myself from anything. I was terrified of dying as a result of no one listening or responding to my needs and had a warranted fear of being put into a mental institution for the same reasons. In a nutshell, I had become mentally ill from trying to prove to everyone that I wasn't mentally ill. Understandably, I was left with appreciable anger and a deep level of distrust towards all medical professionals in general.

And then there was the very real physical torture of the illness itself. Being unable to move for such a long period of time felt comparable to being confined to a straitjacket within a padded room, although my experience came with additional physical suffering. Within some prisons, solitary confinement is used as punishment for inmates. However this practice is prohibited under international law to last for more than 15 days as, beyond this time frame it is constituted as inhuman and degrading (United Nations, 2020).

I had endured this severe form of penance without interruption for over three and a half years, having no form of connection with another living thing. The isolation had been so exceptional that I had lost myself entirely, literally forgetting how it felt to be a human being. It's no wonder that I now felt so unbalanced.

I had been left to face every single one of these gruelling circumstances on my own and had the added fear of not knowing what to do or where to go in order to stay alive. For such a long period of time, I had felt high levels of desperation and panic every single day over being unable to find a way out of my insufferable situation. I was now, still living with the belief that if I didn't get 'it' right I was going to die or worse, never get better. It was very strange to be consciously aware of the fact that I had my health back while simultaneously living with these paralysing fears.

My days continued to be very regimented. I placed rules and restrictions on myself just as I had done for so many previous years, believing that without them I wouldn't be OK. I was constantly worrying about how I was feeling and what messages my body was sending to me. If I experienced any of my remaining symptoms during the day I would question and analyse them, just as I used to. I felt that if I stopped the battle, I would be in danger. I was holding on tight, but to what, I did not know.

During one of my therapy sessions, I created the perfect imagery to illustrate how I was feeling. I pictured myself on my hands and knees, pushing a heavy breeze block with all of my might. I could see it moving inch by inch down a dirt path that stretched far out into the distance. At the same time, I could feel someone with their hands on my shoulders. When I turned around there was a line of twenty people all linked to each other, pulling me backwards as hard as they could. The block was moving ever so slowly forward, inch by inch, only to be dragged back again and again. The unrelenting struggle was incredibly demoralising for me.

I also had many specific experiences that could be regarded as individual traumas. One of these was when the CPAP mask was first put on my face to assist with my breathing difficulties. At that moment I had believed that I was going to suffocate to death. The awful sensation was then extended out to every consecutive day thereafter during the eight months that I had used the device. Even though, by then, I had become aware that it wouldn't actually kill me, the severity of the oxygen deprivation was harrowing enough. Before I had confronted and worked through this disturbance in therapy, I hadn't even been able to think about the mask without it causing me severe distress. This included remembering the smell of it, the sound it made when the tube moved around or looking at pictures of anyone else wearing one.

Feeling all of those layers of trepidation and pain whilst not being able to verbalise my level of suffering was what had kept the trauma locked inside for years. This utter lack of expression of any emotion during the most tumultuous time of my life had compounded my condition even further. It was the sheer physical and mental oppression that had caused the most damage.

Normally, our brains naturally process all of the events that happen to us on a day to day basis. This allows us to decipher when something is a memory of what has happened to us in the past. However, when a person has post-traumatic stress disorder, they live with their past traumas as if they exist in the present moment.

All that I had incurred during the final years of my illness had been too traumatic to process properly during the time that it had happened. Without my awareness, my subconscious mind believed that I was still living during the worst part of my existence. Unconsciously, I was living each day as though I was still back in that bed, lacking power over myself, fearing for my safety and my life. My emotional state in the present was directly linked to those past events. This was the reason why I wasn't able to cope with low levels of everyday stress.

Whenever I had these debilitating feelings, I was told to accept them, be kind and understanding to myself, recognise where they were coming from (the past) and try to observe them without becoming overly involved. My therapist explained to me that as the brain properly dealt with the old memories during therapy there would, slowly but surely, begin to be room for everyday life to creep back in. It would take time, especially because my suffering had been so drawn out. I had to be patient with myself and my mind to slowly reprocess the immense amount of traumatic memories.

That was easier said than done. I wanted to live my life but instead felt that I was wasting precious time on top of all the years that had been stolen from me. The months were slipping by, and I was still unable to feel free. I wondered if my trauma might be too long and complex to ever work through. Just as before, I wished that I could be given a crystal ball to tell me when it would all be over.

Up until now, I had been permanently existing in one continuous emotional flashback. Because of that, it had been impossible for me to comprehend that all of my emotions were, indeed, a reaction to past events. Even after I had learned about flashbacks, being told that all of my seemingly very real and devastating emotions were simply a deception of the mind was quite disturbing and hard for me to believe. But slowly, as the months passed, I started to recognise the truth in those words.

At first it was more of a questioning of my perceived reality. Then, as I began to have fleeting moments of clarity that grew in quantity and length over time, I developed the ability to distinguish between intensely distorted reactions and genuine emotions. It took time and effort, but once I was able to recognise where they were coming from, I could then observe my perceptions for what they were, disentangling myself from the ensnaring grasp they had over me. I learned to be my own greatest support, soothing my past self whenever the debilitating feelings arose.

One of my greatest sources of comfort during my darkest hours, when I had been completely alone, unable to move or speak at all, had been my imagination. At that time, along with my many other waking dreams, I would occasionally envision my future-self visiting me completely healed. 'She' would sit by my bedside, hold my hand

and tell me that one day I would be well. The me from the future would tell myself: 'Keep going, keep fighting, don't give up, you *will* find a way out and everything will be OK.' I had always become extremely emotional when picturing this, almost believing that it was real. I would wonder if it could possibly be the me from the future coming back in order to impart this message, knowing that it was exactly what I needed in order to keep going.

In one particular therapy session, I was asked to carry out this precise exercise, without any awareness on the therapist's behalf of the meaningfulness behind it. And so I went and sat by my past self's side and held on to her hand, just as I had already envisioned that it would happen. I told her to be strong, to not give up, I would be well and everything I wished for would come to be. I said it in the same manner that I had pictured myself doing when I was still immobilised. I told my past self that I was safe now and everything was OK. I had succeeded by using all of my determination and never giving up. It was such a poignant moment for me. I like to think that on some level I really was able to revisit myself and relay the information that I had desperately needed in order to keep on fighting.

Alongside going to therapy I began to visit the local gym. While I was there, I worked on building up my muscles by using different exercise equipment and taking regular yoga classes. The yoga was very beneficial to me as it helped to balance my mind as well as my body. Feeling stronger physically gave me a strength of self again after all of the years that I had spent feeling so weak. Over the next six months, my energy levels continuously improved until I was finally rid of all of my lasting physical symptoms. I believe that this was partly due to the exercise, but also to the tablets reducing my iron deficiency, the simple passing of time and the gradual transformation of my mental health.

Eventually, I felt ready to begin volunteering at a performing arts centre once a week. My responsibilities consisted of no more than collecting tickets from patrons and rubbish from tables but even these simple acts were a lot for me to handle. Nevertheless, as time passed, I was able to witness the gradual growth of my confidence and capabilities. It was as if the heavy fog that had descended over me was finally lifting and, little by little, I was able to see the world more clearly again. The bubble began to dissolve, the haziness dissipate, and my existence come back into focus.

After spending eight months in therapy in which I made some meaningful yet small improvements, I decided that it was time to take another trip away. My reasoning was based upon the notion that I would only be able to truly find my inner strength and autonomy through my active participation in the world. This time I joined a volunteer program in a yoga and personal development retreat in Koh Phangan, Thailand.

The centre had a variety of classes and workshops that I could attend every day. During one of them in particular, I was able to release a facet of my PTSD almost entirely, all within a two-hour timespan. Before attending the class, I had no expectations. The facilitator played recorded music and live instruments to elicit a wide range of emotions while participants were asked to lay down in a room in the dark. However, the key to its success was that we were allowed or rather, encouraged to express as much emotion as we desired, in any form that came to us. We were given total freedom.

About halfway through the process, I began to scream like I had never screamed before. What was released from my body that day were the deep guttural sounds that I had needed but been unable to voice during all of the years I had felt utterly powerless. The noises were so loud and so strong that, at some point, it became necessary for me to stand up from where I lay in the middle of the room and bellow them out as forcefully as possible. The fearful screaming then transformed itself into a powerful yell. The final and most effective roar of a sound to come out of me lasted for what seemed like an eternity but was probably closer to a whole minute.

From that moment forth, I no longer carried the bulk of that crushing burden of repression that the medical profession had inflicted upon me. I had let out almost all of it on that one day. Along with that, the terror I felt of the possibility of being attacked at any moment vanished.

It was this exercise of self-will, in combination with my avid participation in the two month program and my exposure to all of the other participants that allowed me to begin to establish trust in myself, others and the world once more. In volunteering, I gained a sense of value and competency. I met people who I could relate to and, with their unintentional help, learned to communicate properly and to be myself whilst in their company.

During the two months that I spent in Thailand it was brought to my conscious awareness that I was no longer alone in the world, but in actuality there was warmth, kindness and opportunity for connection all around me. As my suffering diminished, there became space for other genuine emotions. The coldness I had previously felt in my heart melted away to be replaced with love. Once I returned home, I was able to make the monumental steps of moving out from my mum's house and getting a part-time job working as a waitress. The feeling of being self-sufficient was indescribably satisfying.

Unfortunately, no matter how remarkable the changes had been, there were other elements of my mental health condition that remained firmly intact. The extremity of my lasting emotional flashbacks made it impossible for me to work more than three days a week. Although I was no longer afraid of being attacked or overpowered, I still felt as though I was exposed and vulnerable to an unsafe world. Therefore, I had to remain aware or some unforeseen atrocity could take place. The only moments that this sensation eased was while spending time with others as they felt like a source of protection from these unreasonable fears. While in another person's presence, I also avoided the trigger of isolation.

In my attempts to evade these debilitating feelings, I remained involved in a romantic relationship with someone even when their influence had become emotionally harmful and toxic. It took some time for me to realise the damage that this was causing to my already low self-worth. Once I had taken the painful but necessary steps to disentangle myself from the unhealthy bond, I knew that it was paramount that I find a way to unravel these deep-seated fears. Soon afterwards, I flew out to Thailand again, to the same location as I had visited the year before. I held high hopes in finding another unconventional and equally as powerful treatment method that would induce similar results.

As luck would have it, I did. The next pivotal experience was actually very similar to the first as this process of emancipation came about, once again, through me screaming from the top of my lungs. It happened during one of the sessions of a six-day breathwork retreat. This time the expression initially focused on all of the painful physical experiences and resulting emotional trauma that I had sustained during those agonising years. It took approximately half an hour for me to release the majority of this suffering.

The purpose of my momentous howling then moved on to the lack of confidence and vulnerability that I constantly felt. During the next half hour, I yelled as the pit of my stomach began to fill with determination and self-belief. Towards the end, the sounds resounded throughout the hall in a clear expression of anger and, with that, grew a feeling of empowerment that had been hidden away for far too long.

When I walked out of the retreat that day, every step I took felt a little lighter than the last. So much built-up anguish had been released from my body within one session of screaming. With my new sense of inner strength, I realised that it was I who had the resources necessary to handle anything that came my way.

Upon that revealing realisation, my viewpoint shifted dramatically. For the first time in years, I perceived the energy of the universe to be working with me instead of conspiring against me which fostered a feeling of trust in both the present moment and in the future. I arrived home a changed person yet again. My anxiety levels had decreased significantly and, because of this, I was able to immediately find a full-time job with a higher level of responsibility. Gone were the days where I allowed others to walk all over me. I had gained a renewed sense of self-regard and could, once again, hold my head high.

Despite me reaping the benefits of these monumental improvements, another element of my subconscious mind still remained firmly rooted in the past. This part of me was unconvinced that the fight for my life was actually over or that I could now rest. I continued to live with intense feelings of terror that if I stopped struggling, I would never find my way out of the darkness. Everything I did was undertaken with relentlessly high levels of stress and pressure as I ran to escape the clutches of that mythical demon.

It was only when I began to truly recognise and honour my fear, allowing it and giving it space to be fully felt, that it began to shrink on its own. Each time I felt the panic arise, I would listen to what it had to say with empathy, as if it was another person. The more love and kindness I showed it, the more it seemed to diminish. Whenever I stopped pushing my emotions away, I wouldn't need to convince myself that the battle was over as, in those moments, the power behind that fear was removed. I was gradually changing my internal story and by doing so, unshackling myself from the burdensome monster that had been weighing me down for so long.

There were still many situations that evoked feelings of excessive isolation. Even though I was now able to value periods of time spent within my own company, if I remained by myself for too long, the panic would set in. To clarify, when this happened, I didn't feel lonely but rather extremely vulnerable and overwhelmed. When I was triggered, I quickly began to relive the disturbing realities from the past; having to cope with all of the turbulence utterly alone even when it reached past the point of endurance, having no one to turn to for help when I felt sheer terror and hysteria and feeling that deep desolate aching in my soul for any kind of human contact. A part of me still equated being alone with being unsafe and defenceless.

And so I made a third and final journey to that magical healing island, in order to let go of one more aspect of the ill, vulnerable girl I had once been. I had full faith in the two month trip's potential and it was not to disappoint me. While taking part in another week-long breathwork retreat I became consciously aware that I had been retaining this piece of the equation on purpose, in order to protect myself. My subconscious mind had believed that, by holding onto it, I would remain vigilant to a certain degree at all times. It was the appreciation of this truth that allowed me to become open enough to relinquish the majority of that fear and pain. I accomplished this by engaging in the same expressive medium as I had for the last two years.

During the rest of the trip I bore witness to the monumental changes that were taking place within me. Instead of seeking out the company of others all the time, I now craved time spent in solitude. I went to the beach on my own most days and stayed there for hours, swimming, sunbathing and taking walks along the water's edge. Each night when I went out to dinner, I took pleasure in the quiet of my own company. When I travelled solo to the north of the country, my old feelings of panic did not accompany me there. In their place, I felt a growing sense of freedom. Within this spaciousness, I found that there was room for a sense of ease, happiness and even excitement for a life lived without fear. It was in this last shift that I was able to stop continuously living in my past and find my place within the present.

In spite of all of the layers of mental suffering that I have already removed, I still have moments in which I feel unsettled. But because of all the progress I have made, these times of insecurity are happening nowhere near as often as they had previously and when they do occur, are not nearly as intense as they used to be. The difference now is that even when I am in the midst of a difficult emotion, my core strength remains intact. Instead of immediately grasping at anything I can in order to avoid these all-consuming feelings, I am now able to ride the wave of my involuntary reaction until it passes. I understand that, to attain true liberation from my suffering, I will need to continue on my path of acceptance of every facet of this experience. I trust that with time and perseverance, I will reach my destination.

The aftermath - My visa photo for Bali.

Coming out of the fog.

Giving my thanks.

Making new friends in Thailand.

Seeing, hearing, smelling, feeling: I am alive.

EPILOGUE
AN UNEXPLAINABLE REALITY

I find it incredible to have fully recuperated from such a long time spent in an exceedingly debilitated state. The last doctor to visit me in my bed told my mum that even if it had been possible to eradicate the diseases, my body could have never recovered from the level of devastation it was in. And yet here I am today, functioning as a healthy individual. During the last years that I was ill, I used to say that I had forgotten how it felt to be well. Now I can remember. I can finally declare that I am one hundred percent healed. I no longer have Lyme disease or any other pathogen and my brain, heart, stomach, breathing, energy and stamina are all in a state of balance once again.

As a result of the illness itself, along with its lengthy aftermath, over ten years of my life passed by without much of my participation in them. At first this was devastating to me. I had to go through a sort of grieving process for the time that had been lost. I have now thankfully come to terms with it and instead, understand how marvellous it is to be able to live in this present moment. I could so easily be dead and in the ground right now. The simple fact that I have a future to create fills me with gratitude every single day.

I still, to this day, experience born-again virgin moments, although they have become far less frequent now. As time passes, I am becoming more and more reaccustomed to this world. But every so often I will come across something 'new' and will then become immediately aware of how lucky I am to be alive.

When I use the word *alive*, I don't mean for it to signify the continuance of my existence but rather that I am full of vitality. A considerable amount of time has passed and yet I have never stopped noticing and feeling a sense of awe over the beauty that is all around me. I treasure so many seemingly mundane occurrences and never fail in those moments to express my appreciation for them. There is so much in the world that is worth living for and I have the fortunate gift of being able to recognise that.

Books that recount personal traumatic experiences will so often end with earnest statements about how appreciative the writer feels for his or her particular misfortune and why they wouldn't be the person they are today without it. When I read those assertions in the past, I tended to wonder if what they were saying was all a bit contrived in order to help that person come to terms with his or her encountered atrocities. I, myself, still cannot attest to being grateful for my ordeal. Nevertheless, it was my path to acceptance of the past that helped to restore my emotional well-being in the end. I now view my experience as a journey with each distinctive part being equally as remarkable and significant as the other. I do not define what took place as either good or bad but simply 'what was' and an invaluable part of what makes me who I am.

If I was given a magic time travelling machine I would, of course, return immediately to the first day that I felt unwell and tell doctors to test me for Lyme disease. If I had been prescribed the required medicine in time, my body would have healed quite quickly. These things aside, if it was possible to talk with my past self during the years that I was ill, I would tell 'her' that she must never allow anyone else to determine what is best for her, no matter what professional title they hold.

In regard to all of the snide remarks, I would advise my past self to attempt to ignore them. Sadly, I realise that because of the sheer magnitude that I would receive over time, that suggestion might be unmanageable to keep up day after day. Regardless of this, I would say to her that she should never doubt her physical illness for one second or that she would one day return to full health. Instead, I would tell her to only ever listen to her own heart and believe in her own personal power. These invaluable lessons are hindsights that I would not have learned without having sustained the trials and tribulations of my illness.

Most of my friends and family, through no fault of their own, had no idea how to correctly respond to my unique situation. Whenever I attempted to speak with them about how unbearable it was for me, their collective reaction was to sugar coat my predicament, thereby discounting the severity of what I was going through, and then change the subject.

If I was offered that time machine, I would make a special trip to each of the people who cared about me to share with them the solace that they could provide by listening to everything I said with an open heart and trusting my words to be true. There was nothing concrete that my loved ones could have done for me. Merely letting go of all judgement and taking the time to try and put themselves in my shoes would have helped me so much. This simple act of kindness would have been like a medicine to me while I was starving for these two things.

Because of the countless abhorrent encounters I had with the medical system, I continued to live with a pronounced distrust of all doctors for a long duration after I had become well. I don't believe that a time machine could help this matter. Be that as it may, if any medical professional happens to be reading, I implore them, in place of their hasty assumptions in regarding an illness as merely psychosomatic, to instead respond by listening and making a proper attempt to understand and acknowledge their patient's symptoms. In doing so it could be possible for them to discover the real causal factor behind the body's continuing dysfunction. At the very least, they would become an invaluable source of support to their patients. I had never personally considered writing a book about my experience but every time I told my story the listener would become utterly captivated and, many times, moved to tears. More often than not, after I finished, they would say to me, 'You must share your story. It could do so much good.' At first, I thought, 'Nah, I don't think so. People wouldn't be interested.' But as the list of people proposing that I document my journey grew, I began to see the plausibility of their point of view.

I started to write but had to stop soon after because I could not yet face the details of what had happened to me. In revisiting my past, I had to confront many painful memories and assimilate them into my personal timeline. It was only when I had already been receiving counselling for several months that I decided to try for the second time. It seemed to be the right moment for me to do this in conjunction with all of my therapeutic pursuits and actually ended up becoming a part of my healing. During the creative process, I was able to unearth and disencumber myself from emotions that I previously had the inability to express, such as anger, indignation, desperation and hopelessness.

However, I did not make this record solely for my own catharsis. I became passionate about sharing my story in order to help others who find themselves in a similar situation to my own. If I could reach out and help even one person who is currently living with the burden of having ME, Lyme disease or any other comparable illness (including long COVID), it would mean more to me than anything else that I could possibly achieve in my lifetime.

I hope that through reading my personal battle with this insufferable disease they may no longer feel so alone in their struggle. Perhaps my specific case could serve as proof that despite the adversity we must suffer there is hope, a chance for the pain to end and for life to begin again. I'm not going to say that my journey was easy because it most certainly was not. I can completely empathise with anyone who feels that their personal struggle is too much to bear to consider one more approach. Yet by relaying my story, I hope that it might reignite their fire, the one that has possibly all but fizzled out by now. I have decided not to be retested for Lyme disease, Epstein-Barr virus or any of the other co-infections that were previously found to be active in my body. My reasoning is based upon the fact that my renewed state of health is due, in entirety, to the power of my mind. If a single test was to come back positive, each of my firmly established convictions would be wiped out in one fell swoop and the all-encompassing fear could then easily reinstate itself into its former position. I will never entertain the possibility of that happening.

You may be curious to know whether I consider myself to have had ME since it was eventually verified that I had Lyme disease. That name provides a label for a profusion of real physical symptoms, most of which I had; so yes. However it does not answer the burning question of why they exist in the first place. I was lucky enough to receive this in the form of my Lyme diagnosis. This important discovery was only made possible because of my own persistence and determination. If I had been listened to properly, if my symptoms had been given appropriate consideration, if there was more research, more knowledge, and more testing being provided, this book would have never been written as my personal story would have been strikingly different.

ME happens to be twice as common as Multiple Sclerosis. However, it receives one of the least amounts of medical research funding; almost 50 times less than MS from the world's leading research organisation; The National Institutes of Health (Brea, 2017). Psychological explanations for the disease have unfortunately held back biological research. It is my strong belief that one day, when medicine has evolved enough to be able to quickly and easily identify the cause(s), the term 'ME' will become obsolete.

Research that was carried out back in 2015 by scientists in the Center for Infection and Immunity at Columbia University has provided indisputable evidence that ME triggers a distinctive immune response in the body. Those with the diagnosis were shown to have immune systems that were actively defending their bodies against some sort of infection (Columbia University, 2015). So, there you have it, in black and white; a person with ME has a quantifiable illness. There can be no mistaking these findings.

Yet there are people all over the world who must continue to face constant unwarranted opposition and ridicule. I am personally aware of one such individual who is in a remarkably similar physical state to that which I was in not so long ago. She is, at the present moment, residing within a psychiatric hospital. Although she has a plethora of real physical symptoms, the only treatment being dispensed to her is for her mental health. Her situation disturbs and infuriates me to such an extent that I cannot bear to think about it.

I had spent an incalculable amount of energy attempting to escape a fate as diabolical as this. However, when the magic finally happened, when I made the impossible possible, it was no longer about trying hard or believing harder in order to get it right. It was simply the way it was going to be. There was no other alternative. I altered my reality without wishing, asking or willing it after realising that under no circumstances could I live one more day in that deplorable state. I had to fully embody the changes I wanted to see.

My intention was key to the success of that pivotal moment. In saying to myself that my body was already healed, I let go of any desperation to be well, therefore eliminating all parts of me that were in doubt of its attainability. Once I surrendered to that idea, all of my psyche was in agreement. From that point on, I no longer analysed how my healing was going to happen or when it would manifest as, in my mind, it already had. I began to do what I wanted without taking any consequences into consideration.

This method deviated from when I had first attempted to be the girl that fell in the pond. In that instance I had thought that by believing in the mission wholeheartedly, I would have a chance of suppressing any repercussions before they began. Yet I had paid attention to them as soon as they materialised, viewing them as irrefutable proof that my undertaking was an impossibility. It also stood in stark contrast to the medical system's recommended treatment of graded exercise, as in this technique the focus remains on asking the body to accomplish something physically impossible while ignoring its cries for help. My tactic was never about pushing myself on any level. It instead concentrated on creating a metamorphosis; a circumstance that is rare but fully attainable. One that any individual can accomplish as long as they succeed in having the right frame of mind. My personal story can be paralleled with that of the 'pond girl's' in that a prognosis that was deemed impossible by doctors and their medical tests had become an unexplainable reality within a matter of moments. Although clearly, if I had never taken the initiative to create the events that occurred, my miracle, as I call it, would have never taken place. Without my resourcefulness, strength and self-belief over the months succeeding, I wouldn't be where I am today. In these regards, I can compare myself to the stage four cancer victim who had regained his health by taking matters into his own hands. In making my demands, I stopped waiting for an answer to find me and became the solution, taking my personal power back in the process.

Once I had released the majority of the trauma from my past, I was able to view my reality in a whole new light. I was aware of being afforded a fresh start, a chance to create an entirely new existence. In place of the panic and fear that I had felt for so long, there came a sense of calm and ease. Instead of hopelessness there was now space for possibility. As human beings, we tend to carry out our lives according to how we perceive the world around us. With this growing sense of trust, I began to embody the life that I had so long wished for.

As I gradually found my place within the world again my mum also began to find hers. She had lived selflessly for years on end; giving up her life in order to try and bring mine back. In that process, the importance of listening to her own needs had sadly been lost along the way. Once the struggle was over, she was able to focus on regaining her happiness and her centre. Through spending quality time with herself, participating in uplifting activities, and resuming full-time employment she began to recreate her own life as she wished it to be. It also gave her a deep sense of satisfaction to be witness to my own continuing progression.

When I first regained my vitality, I had a great desire to participate in any and every adventure that came my way, the more exciting, the better. There was a discernible eagerness inside of me to make up for all of the lost time. I felt happiest whenever given the chance to dance to loud and invigorating music, travel to some far and distant land, look out onto a spectacular view in nature; any event that provided me with a sense of exhilaration. But what made each experience really special was when it was shared with the people I loved. It was in those moments that my heart would overflow with joy.

As I began to find my footing, this enthusiasm for life gradually evolved so that now my sense of fulfilment comes much more from the many simplicities in day to day life, such as having a meaningful conversation with a close friend, sitting quietly with myself in nature, feeling the slowness of my rhythmic breath flowing through me in my yoga practise, or taking some time out during an average day in order to simply observe how truly lucky I am to be alive.

There is a palpable sense of freedom that comes from having full confidence in your own body's ability to continuously function in a state of equilibrium. I am now able to do whatever I please, whenever I want to, but even more importantly, I feel totally at ease in this level of complete trust. Having the awareness that there is no longer a need to fight for my physical health holds so much power. The huge amount of energy that was previously lost in this all-encompassing battle is now used to live my life, taking pleasure in all its richness.

I am currently living in a creative and vibrant city that is surrounded by rolling hills, with the ocean situated only a few streets away from my house. I feel at home here and treasure the beautiful connections that I have created with like-minded people. I work as a psychotherapist and energy healing practitioner, helping others on their journeys of transformation. Because of all that has transpired in my life, I am able and more than willing to be fully present while holding space for each of their processes. From this place they are given the opportunity to explore the depths of their traumas without any restrictions, finding compassion for themselves and all that they have endured. Being able to provide a safe and caring environment where individuals can experience true and lasting healing gives me an immense sense of fulfilment. My goal for the future is to set up a program that empowers people who are trapped in a long-term illness to manifest their own healing. I can think of nothing more valuable to do with my time than this.

I spent over an entire decade consumed by my illness. When I look back over the ordeal, it seems like a previous life as it exists in such contrast to the one I am now able to lead. I feel a sense of freedom like I never have before, because I am fully aware of the power I have over my own destiny. I never could have imagined, in all of my wildest dreams, that the aforementioned events would have happened to me. Nobody ever would. I have been to hell and back and have the passport stamp to prove it. Even still, I appreciate just how lucky I am to write those words: I have been to hell... AND BACK.

ACKNOWLEDGEMENTS

Mom: First and foremost, I want to thank YOU. You were my constant companion, my cheerleader, my strength when it was lacking and my voice when I couldn't speak. You took care of me, you loved me and you listened with remarkable empathy. You were always patient and always kind. From the very first day until the very last you believed in me against all odds and remained right by my side every step of the way. For that I want to thank you from the bottom of my heart.

Dad: Your tremendous generosity, support and magnitude of understanding mean the world to me. I cherish the fact that you are only ever a phone call away. Thank you for being my father and my friend.

To my aunts and uncles: I will always remember your immense contribution. You made it possible for me to keep trying. Without this opportunity I would have been completely lost.

I hold the utmost gratitude and respect for every single health practitioner who is willing to suspend judgement, take their patients' accounts into full consideration and attempt to come up with innovative solutions, instead of simply following what was set out for them in their textbooks. I admire every one of you who feels passionate about and yearns to discover the real reason for your patients' presenting symptoms while taking a genuine interest in helping them to return to a full and happy life. This includes nurses, doctors, hospital staff, alternative medicine practitioners, therapists...

(the list could go on). Without naming any names, I would like to express my sincere appreciation to all of those with whom I was fortunate enough to come into contact with. For your unquestioning belief, tenacious spirit and exceptional level of compassion and care, I want to thank you.

RESOURCES

<u>Myalgic Encephalomyelitis:</u>

Action for M.E.
www.actionforme.org.uk

The Hummingbirds' Foundation for M.E. (HFME) www.hfme.org
(In my opinion, the best website by far. It is run by and for people
with ME and provides so much valuable information and
resources. Look for a link to the book: Caring for the M.E. Patient
by Jodi Bassett. I can personally recommend it as a great read for
anyone who cares enough to want to truly understand the illness
and support someone inflicted with ME in the best way possible. It
is wonderful for carers, family members, friends, doctors and other
medical professionals. It includes a seven-page section entitled: 'So
you know someone with M.E.?'. This is a great handout to provide
to anyone who wants to learn how they can help.)

www.hfme.org/findingagooddoctor.htm
(Part of the HFME website. A strong resource for guiding
someone with ME through finding a doctor and obtaining the right
testing.)

The ME Association
www.meassociation.org.uk

ME Research UK
www.meresearch.org.uk

M.E. Support UK
www.mesupport.co.uk

Lyme disease:

Lyme Disease Action
www.lymediseaseaction.org.uk

LymeDisease.org
www.lymedisease.org

Lyme Disease UK
www.lymediseaseuk.com

www.lymenet.org/BurrGuide200810.pdf
(A wonderfully thorough guide for diagnosis and treatment of Lyme disease.)

Highly respected labs and tests (Lyme disease & viruses):

Immunosciences Lab., Inc: 822 S. Robertson Blvd., STE. 312, Los Angeles, CA 90035 USA. Tel: +01 310 657 1077.
-Viral Panel Comprehensive
-Lyme multi-peptide ELISA assay (IgM and IgG)
-Lyme disease by Western blot (IgM and IgG)

InVitaLab: Hammfelddamm6, 41460 Neuss, Germany.
Tel: +49 2131 125 9690.
-MELISA Lyme borreliosis

IGeneX, Inc: 795 San Antonio Road, Palo Alto, CA 94303.
Tel: +01 800 832 3200.
-Lyme immunofluorescence assay
-Lyme Western blot (IgM and IgG)
-Multiplex PCR (serum and whole blood)

GcMAF/Goleic:

Cancer Tutor
www.cancertutor.com/gcmaf-potential-cure
(Addresses the controversy over GcMAF and provides useful
information about the immune system boosting supplement.)

http://vimeo.com/41377604
(Video explaining GcMAF and how it works.)

PTSD:

Mind www.mind.org.uk/information-support/types-of-mental-
health-problems/post-traumatic-stress-disorder-ptsd/#

Royal College of Psychiatrists
www.rcpsych.ac.uk/healthadvice/problemsdisorders/posttraumati
cstressdisorder.aspx

MEpedia me-pedia.org/wiki/Post-traumatic_stress_disorder (Study
focusing specifically on people with ME/CFS that have PTSD
caused by the effects of stigma by medical professionals and
others.)

Controversy:

For ME/CFS:

Is ME/CFS a medical illness or a psychosomatic condition?:

www.meassociation.org.uk/2016/06/the-all-in-the-mind-myth-of-myalgic-encephalomyelitischronic-fatigue-syndrome-nursing-in-practice-27-june-2016

qz.com/884658/are-chronic-fatigue-syndrome-ibs-and-crohns-disease-really-all-in-the-mind-a-psychosomatic-disease-diagnosis-is-a-doctors-way-of-saying-i-dont-have-a-clue

www.nature.com/news/biological-underpinnings-of-chronic-fatigue-syndrome-begin-to-emerge-1.21721

www.dailymail.co.uk/health/article-2972865/Proof-yuppie-flu-real-illness-Study-finds-chronic-fatigue-commonly-seen-professionals-not-just-mind.html

Whether a combination of graded exercise and psychological therapy really works:

www.meassociation.org.uk/2017/08/the-daily-mail-why-are-doctors-and-patients-still-at-war-over-m-e-15-august-2017

www.telegraph.co.uk/news/health/12033810/Its-time-for-doctors-to-apologise-to-their-ME-patients.html

www.hfme.org/cbtandgeteffectsc.htm

For Lyme disease:

Whether chronic Lyme disease is real and can be treated for:

https://lymediseaseassociation.org/videos/contagion-chronic-lyme-controversy-videos/

www.bbc.co.uk/news/magazine-34579423

globallymealliance.org/illness-no-one-believes-in-lyme-disease

Testing:
www.tiredoflyme.com/4-reasons-a-lyme-test-will-come-back-negative-even-if-a-person-truly-has-lyme-disease.html

Diagnosis:
sheamedical.com/how-to-recognize-what-your-doctor-may-miss%E2%80%93and-how-to-find-real-treatment

www.dailymail.co.uk/health/article-4895432/Yolanda-Hadid-says-Lyme-disease-misdiagnosed-ME.html

danielcameronmd.com/misdiagnosing-lyme-disease

www.dailymail.co.uk/health/article-4810754/How-tiny-tick-bite-left-rugby-hero-needing-heart-surgery.html

www.dailymail.co.uk/health/article-5035499/If-Stephen-Hawking-work-t-you.html

REFERENCE LIST

American Myalgic Encephalomyelitis and Chronic Fatigue Syndrome Society. (n.d.). Exercise. https://ammes.org/exercise/

Banerjee, J. (2021, August 30). In oneself lies the whole world. Krishnamurti Foundation India. https://kfikolkata.org/2021/08/30/in-oneself-lies-the-whole-world/

Brea, J. (Director). (2017). Unrest [Film]. Shella Films. Retrieved March 2020, from https://www.youtube.com/watch?v=iTC0y4l1Jgc.

Columbia University's Mailman School of Public Health (2015, February 7). Scientists Discover Robust Evidence That Chronic Fatigue Syndrome Is a Biological Illness. https://www.mailman.columbia.edu/public-health-now/news/scientists-discover-robust-evidence-chronic-fatigue-syndrome-biological

HubPages (2014, July 15). Complex PTSD symptoms and treatment. https://www.hubpages.com/health/Complex-PTSD-Symptoms-and-Treatment

Lymedisease.org. (n.d.). About Lyme Disease. https://www.lymedisease.org/lyme-basics/lyme-disease/about-lyme/

Lymedisease.org. (n.d.). Lyme disease symptoms. https://www.lymedisease.org/lyme-basics/lyme-disease/symptoms

ME Awareness: Words and Pictures (2013, February 3). Dozens of
    everchanging symptoms of Myalgic Encephalomyelitis – ME/CFS
    version.
    https://www.meawarenesspics.blogspot.co.uk/2013/02/there-are-
    so-many-symptoms-of-myalgic.html

M.E or CFS?: Clearing up the confusion (2006-14). http://www.name-
    us.org/MECFSExplainPages/MECFS%20Explained.htm

United Nations Human Rights Office of the High Commissioner (2020,
    February 28). United States: Prolonged Solitary Confinement
    Amounts to Psychological Torture, Says UN Expert.
    https://www.ohchr.org/en/press-releases/2020/02/united-states-
    prolonged-solitary-confinement-amounts-psychological-torture

ABOUT THE AUTHOR

Carly became ill with ME at the age of 24. After making a full recovery, she has become passionate about sharing her story with others. Through her efforts she hopes to raise awareness of ME and, in doing so, lessen the stigma that prevails surrounding an illness that is currently being treated as if it doesn't exist. She also aims to spread the message that each person has the power to create positive change in their lives, no matter how overwhelming their personal adversity may seem.

Carly is happiest when living near the sea. She works as an energy healing practitioner and IFS therapist in Brighton. Visit her website for more info: www.sunrisehealing.co.uk

Printed in Great Britain
by Amazon

26393000R00142